₽·B The Practitioner's Bc

Hands-On Literacy Books for
Classroom Teachers and Administrators

Dorothy S. Strickland
FOUNDING EDITOR, LANGUAGE AND LITERACY SERIES

Celia Genishi and Donna E. Alvermann
LANGUAGE AND LITERACY SERIES EDITORS*

* For a list of current titles in the Language and Literacy Series, see *www.tcpress.com*

DIY Media
in the Classroom

New Literacies Across Content Areas

BARBARA GUZZETTI,
KATE ELLIOTT,
AND DIANA WELSCH

Foreword by Shannon Decker

TEACHERS COLLEGE PRESS

Teachers College, Columbia University
New York and London

Published by Teachers College Press, 1234 Amsterdam Avenue, New York, NY 10027

Library of Congress Cataloging-in-Publication Data

Guzzetti, Barbara J.
    DIY media in the classroom : new literacies across content areas / Barbara Guzzetti, Kate Elliott, and Diana Welsch ; foreword by Shannon Decker.
        p. cm.
    Includes bibliographical references and index.
    ISBN 978-0-8077-5079-7 (pbk. : alk. paper)
        1. Internet in education. 2. Digital media. 3. Content area reading.
    I. Elliott, Kate (Kate F.) II. Welsch, Diana. III. Title.
    LB1044.87.G89   2010
    371.33'44678--dc22   2009049412

ISBN 978-0-8077-5079-7 (paper)

Printed on acid-free paper
Manufactured in the United States of America

17   16   15   14   13   12   11   10   8   7   6   5   4   3   2   1

To Jerry Johns and Mary Lee Smith, who taught me by example excellence in teaching and research, and in memory of Fleure and Chinooks.

Barbara Guzzetti

To Shannon Decker, who taught me how to write well, and to all public school teachers.

Kate Elliott

To Stacie Jane Griffith, who made me realize that it was okay to learn in school.

Diana Welsch

Contents

Foreword

When approached to write this Foreword, I couldn't help but recall when I spoke to graduate education students on do-it-yourself media in schools. I had spent hours that evening answering questions about my students and my teaching experiences. The audience was interested in furthering a broad definition of literacy and forming understandings of various means of communication. In doing so, they had been examining Kate Elliott's and Diana Welsch's zine, an underground self-publication written from a feminist perspective that addressed issues of social justice in the typical in-your-face tone of radical zines.

I remember that some audience members were appalled that as a teacher I would invite such controversial materials into my classroom. They seemed to think that I must be some kind of freak, reckless, or overly interested in getting kids to like me. As our conversation progressed, they painted me as a character lurking within playground shadows, pushing unspeakable corruptions onto unsuspecting innocents.

Others in the audience saw DIY media as a way to bring students' interests into the classroom. But I couldn't help but think of this sort of teaching as a contrived parlor trick: What could we do as educators to make school cool? Yet my message was to honor individual students by acknowledging the media with which they are proficient.

It took me years of teaching and wanting to improve my students' engagement to adopt this strategy. Inviting DIY media into the classroom isn't for the faint of heart. It's an experiment in trust between a teacher and his or her students that requires relinquishing some control to collaboratively design the learning experience. It is daunting at first, but experiencing the fear that comes with such experimentation is worth it in light of the rewards. I believe that to get the most out of students, we teachers need to value students' strengths and not our own. Teachers can be flexible about the texts they use if the objectives are met.

These are the beliefs that led me to try DIY media in my classroom. I gave assignments in which students needed to demonstrate their aptitude, but I would have them choose the medium. Students chose to blog, choreograph and dance historical events, or compose and sing songs that analyzed poetry. It was during one of these presentations that Kate, Diana, and their classmates shared their talent for zines.

I remember the first time I tried this approach. What transpired was truly magical. My students were electrified, and the excitement that rippled throughout the classroom touched even those students who seemed to have checked out long ago. One such young man performed a song that analyzed a poem we had read about the Russian Revolution, complete with guitar accompaniment. Not only did he do the assignment well, but he took pains to bring in equipment that he felt that he needed for the performance. I was amazed by the strides that he took to ensure that his assignment was a success. Using these DIY forms also gave him a chance to showcase his strengths for his classmates. As a result, all of us had a greater appreciation for poetry and for one another. His performance and its message transformed him and his peers in ways that a textbook could not. From that moment forward, I was hooked on allowing DIY media into my classroom.

My experiences raised some questions. Does integrating DIY media into instruction mean that anything goes? How does a teacher distinguish between appropriate and inappropriate DIY media? In my classroom, I strove for balance in offering opinions and presentation styles. Sometimes it worked and sometimes it didn't.

My students and I talked about why it was important to be considerate of others in mediums and messages. For example, Kate and Diana had worked with some of their friends in the class on zines. One girl remarked with a wry smile that they could use their zine to present their ideas on controversial topics to unnerve the more conservative students in the class. So, as a class, we talked at length about what it meant to present one's own ideas while respecting others.

I had these kinds of discussions a lot with my students, and I think that's what kept me out of the school board's line of sight most of the time and made my classroom work so well. It's not that I wanted to silence my students' voices, but rather to not use their voices in ways that stifled others. They wanted to be heard, but they needed to grant one another that same courtesy. That didn't mean that they needed to agree with one another. Because I believed and practiced this philosophy in my classroom, I think I made a difference. I can't recall a time when a student used DIY media just for the sake of self-promotion.

As for the make-school-cool crowd, I hope they will be cautious when incorporating DIY media into classrooms. There are a lot of benefits to including DIY media in classrooms, but there are limitations, too. Although Kate and Diana used a zine format for their school project, making a zine a school assignment partially stripped its power as a mode of expression. It was no longer a real zine that allowed authors to express themselves in unrestricted ways. My requirement for respect may have made the medium of zines appropriate for the classroom, but in the process weakened the mode and therefore the message

As teachers, we can invite different modes of expression into our classrooms, but we must also recognize that classrooms are public, regulated spaces. As such, they will also dictate what ideas can be expressed and how. DIY media is exactly what it says it is—do-it-yourself. Some DIY media like zines are inherently personal—say it yourself, for yourself. When we attempt to bring highly personal DIY media into schools, we may be transforming them into something different.

Nevertheless, I love using DIY media in the classroom. As Barbara, Kate, and Diana suggest, DIY media allow students to transcend boundaries of locale, age, gender, and social class to share their ideas. What more could we as educators want than to encourage diverse discourse? DIY media grant platforms to those who otherwise might not write because they have not had open forums for their voices. The chapters on blogs and wikis, for example, describe how DIY media are well suited for instruction by allowing divergent experiences and ideas to come together.

It is with these words of encouragement in mind that I invite other teachers to consider how the do-it-yourself media presented in the coming pages may be appropriate for their own classrooms. What better way could there be to incorporate the spirit of honoring the individual in teaching than through DIY media?

—Shannon Decker, September 2009

Acknowledgments

We wish to thank the following people who assisted us in the production of this book: Corey Busboom, T. K. Campo, Alan Davis, Deirdre Fischer, Kevin Hagge, Miranda Hantla, Betty Hayes, Jack Hesse, Andrew Jemsek, Deirdre Kelly, Nora Beers Kelly, Quinn Kelly, Chris Lincoln, the Martinez family, Mike Thrall, and Patrick Todd. We also thank Donna Alvermann for her recommendation that we author a book in the Practitioner's Bookshelf series, and for her inspiration. In addition, we acknowledge the contributions of our development editor, Judy Berman, and the continued support of our acquisitions editor, Meg Lemke at Teachers College Press.

Preface

Are you interested in using do-it-yourself (DIY) media to engage adolescents in new literacy practices in these exciting, technologically sophisticated times? Like us, you may have been struck by how deeply engrossed young people can be in creating their own profiles and posting their own or others' videos on their MySpace pages. You may have been impressed by teens writing their life stories in their online journals or sharing their experiences by creating YouTube videos. You may have been surprised that even those students who are otherwise disinterested in or underperforming with traditional forms of literacy can be motivated and articulate in producing these new media texts.

Your observations of young people consuming and producing these DIY media may have left you with some questions, too. You may wonder why these new literate practices are so appealing to students. You may ask how you could incorporate these kinds of DIY media practices in your instruction to make your students more interested and involved in their learning in school.

This book will help you answer those questions. We invite you to explore DIY media with us in these pages. You will learn about their appealing features, discover the literacy skills and abilities that these new media foster, and find some appropriate ways to engage today's students in learning with DIY media.

DEFINING DIY MEDIA AND ADOLESCENCE

We define DIY media broadly as those tools and practices that facilitate creating new media texts, such as a song, an online journal entry, or a video game. In doing so, we address those practices that are entirely noncommercial, as well as those that have a commercial base but facilitate young people's own creations of content. We present those aspects of media literacy that focus on creative production (Greenaway, 2001) or young people's design and implementation of new media, such as web pages, video games, and blogs. These DIY media are ways in which young people critically question commercial media by learning the visual, semiotic, aural, and technological literacies necessary to situate themselves within participatory culture (Peppler & Kafai, 2007a).

We also define adolescence rather broadly. Although we focus mainly on teenagers, many preteens are also experimenting with DIY media and are also instructed in content areas, such as science, social studies, and language arts. There is precedence for thinking broadly about adolescence, which has been defined for literacy assessment purposes as including grades 5–12, when students transition to more sophisticated uses of reading and writing (Salinger, 2007). Broader definitions of adolescence are also promoted by a view of adolescence as not a chronological age range, but rather as a sociocultural construction (Alvermann, 2009), a time of transition in cognitive capacities and social relations that begins in middle school (Intrator & Kunzman, 2009).

THE AUTHORS AS DIYERS

It is with these definitions in mind, and from our own perspectives as DIYers, that we write. Among the three of us, our expertise with DIY media varies, perhaps because our generations and lifestyles are different. Barbara is a professor of literacy education who has been teaching at a university for over 20 years. Diana is a library assistant in an urban public library. And Kate is a full-time graduate student. Barbara is a baby boomer whose first contact with computers came in graduate school in the early 1980s, using large mainframe machines that looked nothing like the laptops of today. Kate and Diana are members of the millennial generation that includes those born since 1980. Millennials like Kate and Diana have grown up with computers and a peer network of technological support, and as a result have had access to a wider range of new literacy practices than past generations. They also are referred to as and are members of the Net Generation (Tapscott, 1998).

Our different generations have influenced how we and our peers have experimented with DIY media, and our unique partnership represents variability in expertise with and perspectives on DIY media. This book is distinctive because it is written from the point of view of those who engage extensively with DIY media who were not long ago adolescents themselves, yet also presents the viewpoint of a literacy researcher who has just begun to become engaged with DIY media. In choosing Shannon Decker to write the Foreword to this book, we also highlight the voice of Kate and Diana's former high school teacher, who experimented with and supported her students' DIY efforts in her language arts/social studies instruction. Our book presents a balance between what young people have to say about DIY media and its appropriate use in classrooms, what a teacher who has incorporated DIY media in content teaching says about it, and what the research on DIY media as literacy practice says. Our personal experiences illustrate the range of DIY media that we discuss in this book and demonstrate the social nature of these new literacies.

BARBARA'S REFLECTIONS ON HER DIY MEDIA PRACTICES

It was Shannon Decker who first told me about Kate and Diana's zine. At that time (about 8 years ago), I didn't know what a zine was and I had never seen or read one. After talking with Kate (and later Diana), I learned that zines are self-publications written and/or edited by independent authors as alternatives to commercial magazines. Zines allow their authors to share their personal thoughts on subjects of interest and importance to them, particularly topics that are not commonly found in the popular press, such as self-injurious behaviors, anorexia, date rape, and homophobia. Zines also allow youth to celebrate art and music and produce their own stories. Kate and Diana shared zines with me and told me where to find them both online and in offbeat places, such as alternative record and book stores.

Although I do not write or edit my own zines, I read, archive, and share them. I've distributed zines on my travels, taking copies with me and leaving them in interesting places that I visit, such as St. Mark's Place in New York City, an area known for DIY (or indie) music and punk rock with its associated artifacts, such as clothing, bands' buttons, and zines. I've passed zines out to teenagers on the subway in London, and I've left them in independent bookstores in Edinburgh. Locally, I share zines with my graduate students who are preservice and inservice teachers to make them aware of both issues of importance to young people and the alternative ways that youth find to express their ideas when those topics are not sanctioned in school or taken up in commercial media.

In addition to consuming and distributing DIY media, I've created my own DIY media by making a page on a social networking site, Facebook. I was prodded to do so by a trusted colleague and longtime friend, Donna Alvermann at the University of Georgia, who solicited her friends by e-mail to join Facebook. I was reluctant because I am busy with other forms of digital communication, so I didn't act on her invitation at first. But then I started receiving e-mail messages that Donna had written on my wall on Facebook! Donna was determined to have me join this online community. I figured that since this was important to her, and because she is important to me, I would appease her and create my own page. So, using a photo of one of my six dogs, I posted my profile on Facebook. Much to my surprise, I quickly discovered that many other colleagues whom I value were also on Facebook. I was soon viewing photos of them and their pets, reading about their travels, and getting recommendations for professional books and YouTube videos. One colleague posted a feminist remix of excerpts from *Buffy the Vampire Slayer* and the *Twilight* movies showing Buffy fighting back against a vampire rather than being seduced by one. In ways like these, sites like Facebook and MySpace enable their users to write and share their life experiences just as online journals do, and to share created or remixed media for their own purposes.

I am also an active resident of the virtual world Second Life, an online site that enables people across the globe to meet and share virtual experiences. With the assistance and encouragement of my treasured colleague Angela Thomas at the University of Sydney, I've created and named an avatar to represent me "in world." I've also created a meeting place, CyberTechs, on my property on a teaching island where I meet my students and teach a class called Teaching and Learning Literacies in Virtual Worlds.

As a newcomer to these new literacies, I am proud of my digital efforts. Praise and encouragement from my friends and colleagues keep me interested in exploring other DIY media. In the coming days, I hope to explore other virtual worlds like WhyVille and Active Worlds to share with my graduate students.

KATE REFLECTS ON HER DIY MEDIA PRACTICES

My experience with DIY media began when I produced my zine in high school. I had Internet access at the time, but my full entrance into online activity had not come yet. The zine I produced with good friends was a fun way to express our personalities, interests, and political viewpoints. Social justice and equality are values that are very important to me, and the zine was the best way for me to share those. Although my opinions have matured since that time, I look back on those memories very fondly. I am still a zine reader, although I have been less engaged in that world than I was years ago.

I have been using online tools like LiveJournal, Facebook, MySpace, and YouTube for years, and they are a part of daily life for me. These social networking sites that I have been using since I began my undergraduate studies have allowed me to connect to friends, family, co-workers, and community organizers. These tools are invaluable to both my work and my personal life. Most people my age are connected through these tools, and we share a common understanding not only of how these tools work, but also how they can work for us in meeting our personal goals.

DIANA REFLECTS ON HER DIY MEDIA PRACTICES

I've been involved with DIY media ever since I was in elementary school. When I was 7 years old, I created a book of my nightmares. Then in 5th grade, some friends and I formed a singing group called the Wildcats, and we recorded ourselves with a portable cassette recorder singing amusing lyrics that we composed to the tunes of popular songs.

In high school, I started contributing to zines, and eventually I wrote and edited my own zine that focused on music and humor. When I was 15, I was in my first real band, where I played drums and guitar, wrote punk rock music, and helped to record and distribute my band's album. At 17, I was asked to join an amazing band as the bass player, and I played with them until I was 21.

Today, I still write and record music with my very talented friend Shawn. I am also a writer of fan fiction (self-authored stories based on other media) based on a video game, Phoenix Wright. I write stories that use the setting of this courtroom mystery game to imagine the characters' romances and conflicts with one another. I post them on a Phoenix Wright fan fiction website called Objection! (www.idletheme.com/objection) for others to read. I also listen to video game music created by video game fans.

I currently work in a library's teen center, where I consume and produce DIY media with teenagers. It's wonderful to get paid to help the teens create comics! The library teens and their DIY creations are my pride and joy.

A PREVIEW OF THE CHAPTERS

As our stories illustrate, we are interested in encouraging learners to explore new media through their contact with one another so that they can customize these formats for their own purposes. When we engage in DIY media, we adopt the underlying ethos that if you cannot find something you like, create it yourself. This book is a by-product of our conversations about DIY media and the need to share with teachers how to use them in schools from the perspective of those who produce them.

We do not address all forms of DIY media or their appealing features simply because there are so many, and the fast-paced nature of new technologies means that even more may develop while this text is in production. Rather, we introduce a variety of DIY media that will acquaint teachers and other readers with these practices and provide some suggestions for appropriately incorporating them into instruction. These suggestions may be a starting point for generating your own ideas for using DIY media for teaching and learning.

To this end, we've structured the chapters by medium. In each chapter, we define and explain the particular genre or genres of DIY media it addresses. We identify some of the literacies that those media foster, and the literate strategies and abilities that young people develop as they engage in these practices. We also provide a brief overview of some of the appealing features of these practices for adolescents. We conclude each chapter with suggestions for using these DIY media in content areas.

We begin our book with an Chapter 1, "Adolescents' DIY Media as New Literacies," which situates DIY media within new digital and print-based literacies and provides a rationale for the need for teachers and other adults working with youth to become familiar with these practices. We describe the benefits that adolescents receive in working with DIY media and situate the topic within current theory on youth culture. Finally, we discuss related issues of access, value, and social justice that impact students' capabilities of engaging in these new literacies and address issues of Internet safety.

In Chapter 2, "Blogs," we define a weblog and describe how blogs function, what blogs contain, and how they are used by teens, including an overview of those blog-hosting sites that are widely read and written by youth. We also describe various types of blogs, and provide examples of and sources of support for classroom blogs and caveats in using blogs in classrooms. Finally, we offer suggestions for using weblogs in teaching in various content areas.

In Chapter 3, "Social Networking and Social Media Sites," we explore the most popular social networking/social media sites in North America—MySpace and Facebook—and describe a related site, Flickr, for photography sharing, which is often incorporated on these sites. We explain the features and functions of these sites, such as comments, messages, and applications. This chapter concludes by describing how the DIY features of these sites could be used appropriately in content classrooms.

In Chapter 4, "Video Games, Machinima, and Virtual Worlds," we introduce video games and three-dimensional environments that adolescents create that make up a large part of youth culture, such as *World of Warcraft*, *The SIMS*, and *Teen Second Life*. We explain how students are enabled to create their own video games by commercial video game companies that provide the tools to extend their games, and how students use this software to create their own films called "machinima." We situate these DIY media in the research on the learning principles reflected in video games and what students learn from their interactions with them, and we provide suggestions for incorporating these media into content teaching.

In Chapter 5, "YouTube and Video Sharing Sites," we explore the Broadcast Yourself phenomenon. In doing so, we describe the websites that host user-generated videos, such as YouTube, Teacher Tube, and Tango, and provide examples of videos made by teens, such as those YouTube videos produced by Global Kids in New York City that focus on international and social problems. We also explain viral videos and discuss related privacy and safety concerns in composing and sharing videos and provide examples of how DIY videos might be used for teaching and learning.

In Chapter 6, "Informational Wikis and Online Resources," we describe online resources and references by starting with wikis, multi-authored online texts such as Wikipedia, and describing how they are used for information-sharing. We introduce other online resources with multiple author content and social networking features. This chapter concludes with suggestions for incorporating these reference tools into content classrooms.

In Chapter 7, "Fan Fiction, Fan Art, and Web Comics," we provide an overview of how young people create art, fan fiction, and comics by using web-based tools and sites. We explain how the Internet makes it possible for comic, cartoon, art, and fiction creators to connect with their readers in ways that are not possible with traditional print media. We discuss fandom, provide a brief history of fan fiction, suggest how it might be useful for writing in classrooms, provide links to websites for creating online DIY media, and offer suggestions for various content areas.

In Chapter 8, "Zines and Indie Music," we explain how young people who cannot find magazines, music, or other publications that address their interests or views create their own. We identify zines as one of the first DIY media and describe how zines are obtained online through Distros (online distribution centers) and offline at record and book stores and at Infoshops. We explore how music can be created, performed, shared, and discussed independently both on- and offline, and we provide suggestions for connecting to adolescents' interests in music in classroom instruction.

In our last chapter, "DIY Media, Assessment, Achievement, and Ethics," we explain the need for authentic assessments that reflect and address these new media literacy skills and abilities. We offer some suggestions for ways that teachers can design their own informal measures. Second, we address ethical issues that impact DIY media. Finally, we provide a description of and a link to our blog for further resources and updates. This chapter refers readers to Appendices, which contain a list of useful resources and a overview of the literacy skills and abilities fostered by DIY media.

We are excited to offer our readers the chance to delve into these DIY media in these pages along with us. We offer ideas for using DIY media in teaching and learning that appropriately recognize the new literate skills and abilities of today's youth. In doing so, we present a glimpse into the literate lives of our millennial youth.

DIY Media
in the Classroom

New Literacies Across Content Areas

CHAPTER I

Adolescents' DIY Media as New Literacies

MySpace, Facebook, Teen Second Life, LiveJournal—these are terms that teachers hear their students talking about with one another. These words identify new forms of communication and literate practice, often referred to as the new literacies (Lankshear & Knobel, 2003). Teens are leaders in exploring and interacting with these new literacies, particularly those print-based or digital practices that allow them to be do-it-yourselfers (DIYers) who create their own literate products. Today's adolescents are "digital natives" (Prensky, 2006) who have grown up with computers and online resources like blogs and wikis. They have had their peers' influence and assistance with these practices to the point that they are almost automatic and natural in their use.

Today's teachers, however, are often "digital migrants" (Prensky, 2006) who have not grown up with these resources, but have had to investigate and become accustomed to them. Hence, teachers who are older than the millennial generation may find it more difficult than their students to become knowledgeable about these informal literacies. Adults often lack the social community of support and encouragement to embrace these literate practices that teenagers find so readily among one another. In fact, busy teachers may have little or no desire to engage in these new literacies themselves and may not find or make the time to do so.

WHY SHOULD TEACHERS CARE ABOUT DIY MEDIA?

Why is it important for teachers to become familiar with these new literacies? One compelling reason is the need to interest and motivate adolescents. In their conversations with teenagers, researchers have documented that many teens, from those underperforming with traditional literacies (Knobel, 2001) to the high-achieving honors and Advanced Placement students (Guzzetti, 2009b), perceive that school is not relevant to their everyday lives. This sense of irrelevancy leads to feelings of alienation and disconnection with academic settings and literacies. Adolescents report learning more about academic topics from their own interactions outside of school on the Internet than they do in their classrooms (Magnifico, 2005). Their feelings of disassociation put adolescents at risk of dropping out. Capitalizing on and incorporating the literate practices that young people engage in outside of school can help to address these negative perceptions that young people often have about instruction.

A second reason to become familiar with the DIY media that adolescents choose to engage in is the need to view millennial students in a different light. Typically, adults take a deficit view of adolescents. To be effective in this new millennium, teachers will need to see their students in a different way—not as less than adults, but as different from adults (Alvermann, 2009).

This model of adolescence acknowledges the "funds of knowledge" (Gonzales, Moll, & Amanti, 2005) that students bring with them to the classroom, such as their cultural backgrounds and their literacy competencies in other settings. Researchers advocate that teachers acknowledge and provide recognition for these new literacy skills and practices (Knobel, 2001). By allowing students to teach their teachers and peers these new literacies, educators can capitalize on students' strengths and acknowledge individuals as capable and articulate people who can inform others.

A third reason for teachers to develop a working familiarity with these practices is to stay current with changing views and innovations. DIY media represent a shift in perspective on literacy from the dominant cognitive model that emphasizes reading to a broader understanding of a range of literacy practices that are situated within social and cultural contexts (Street, 1995). Although the principles of reading and writing have not changed, literacy has shifted from a focus merely on print texts to include the ability to process multimodal text images, including digital texts, lyrical texts, and visual texts (Luke, 2003).

As a result, researchers are attempting to help bridge the gap between adolescents' in- and out-of-school literacies by identifying and describing these informal literacy practices (e.g., Guzzetti & Gamboa, 2005a, 2005b; Mahiri, 2004) and by promoting instruction that incorporates appropriate and relevant new literacies, such as DIY media (Hull & Schultz, 2002). For example, a science teacher experimented with class blogs where students write, read, and peer-review their own murder mysteries where clues represent the forensic concepts and skills that they learned in chemistry class (Guzzetti, in press). English/Language Arts teachers have capitalized on their students' facility with video games by helping their students compose fiction through creating digital game stories (McClay, Mackey, Carbonaro, Szafron, & Schaeffer, 2007). A high school foreign language teacher used the virtual world of Second Life to establish a disco where class members spoke in French to one another as they danced in this virtual world (Collis, 2009).

Teachers who incorporate new media into their instruction in ways like these tend to realize that those who engage in DIY media practices are learning unique new literacy skills and abilities. Some of these new literacy skills and abilities are multitasking, making intertextual ties, designing texts, learning new digital languages, and writing in hybrid forms or creating texts that use both Internet and print texts. These are the new literacy skills and abilities that will be increasingly needed for the 21st-century workforce (Sanford & Madill, 2007). Already, assessments are being developed to measure students' facilities with these new literate skills and abilities (Hammett, 2007).

Finally, we recognize that adolescence is a time of self-explora-
tion and self-discovery. Adolescents try on and test out new identities, perhaps more so than they will at any other point in their
lives. These new literacies of DIY media are inherently interesting
to young people because they enable individuals to represent themselves in alternative ways and create literate products (e.g., blogs,
journals, video games, zines) that reflect their current interests and
changing identities.

Teachers can use DIY media to help students develop their
identities as learners. Students may enact their identities as members of an e-community creating digital game stories, as investiga-
tors of knowledge who blog to share information, or as authors of
online journals written in the foreign language that they are studying in school. By incorporating these new media into their teaching,
teachers acknowledge that students do not stop learning when the
school bell rings (Hull & Schultz, 2002).

ACCESSING AND VALUING NEW DIY LITERACIES

Even as we advocate for instruction that celebrates and embraces
these DIY media practices, we are mindful that not all students have
equal access to engage in them either in or out of school. Too often,
students from low socioeconomic groups, those that are isolated
geographically, and students of color lack access to computers or
do not have up-to-date computers capable of providing access, or
they may lack Internet connections. Access to technology support
is important because even print-based DIY practices may be fa-
cilitated by word processing, e-mail, and Internet networking and
broadcasting. Many young people may be unaware of or unable to
consume and produce these new literacies.

Lack of access leads to another problem related to social justice
—awareness of the value of these new literacies. Adults and young
people who do not engage in DIY media, particularly digital DIY
media, often fail to realize their value. This is such a serious concern that it is has been referred to as the new civil rights issue of the
millennium (Carvin, 2000).

As the new millennium progresses, the literate skills and abilities that are fostered by these DIY practices will become increasingly in demand in tomorrow's workforce. A new global society and

global economy are being fostered by digital literacies, including digital DIY media. Those who lack these skills will be left behind in the world marketplace.

GENDER JUSTICE AND THE NEW LITERACIES

Although students' socioeconomic status impacts their access to and facility with new literacies, researchers have documented that gender also impacts learning both in and out of school (e.g., Mazzarella, 2005; Sanford & Madill, 2007). Gender influences what is socially acceptable learning and what is out of bounds as feminine or masculine practices. Issues of power, exclusivity, and status prevail with the new literacies just as they impact traditional forms of literacy.

Gender Gaps in Mastering New and Old Literacies

Traditional forms of academic literacies have typically been associated with girls' interests and abilities (Skelton, 2001). Although boys resist school literacies where they typically have been less successful than girls, they are becoming literate in new digital literacies outside of school. Young men learn different ways of speaking, listening, viewing, and understanding through their interactions with new technologies (Gee, 2003).

Adolescent boys engage more often and at more sophisticated levels than girls do with new literacies by playing and creating their own video games, making video game music, and engaging in computer-based activities (Sanford & Madill, 2007). In doing so, young men learn a range of skills that will lead to social, economic, communication, and technological value in the workplace (Sanford & Madill, 2007). They are learning these skills in highly complex environments outside of school.

Researchers studying boys developing video games documented both the traditional and new literacy skills that young men learned in creating computer games (Gee, 2003; Sanford & Madill, 2007). These new literacies include how to blend visual and print texts; how to explore new technologies; and, through programming, how to create rules for movement and interaction. Boys enhance their understandings of traditional literacy through using and interpreting literary devices, such as symbolism and contrast in game creation. Boys who create video games enhance their critical thinking abilities by problem solving, reading and understanding rules, decoding meaning systems, and reflecting on strategies.

Cyberbullying and Sexual Harassment

Perhaps one reason that girls participate less in creating video games or online communities is that sexual harassment and cyberbullying are prevalent in online environments. Cyberbullies spread rumors and make threats (*Weekly Reader*, 2007). A recent survey, *The Pew Internet and American Life Project Parents and Teens Survey* (Lenhart, 2007), showed that teenage girls are more likely to be targets of cyberbullying than boys. Older teen girls reported being intimidated online more often than other young people. Adolescents identified some of these harassing behaviors, such as spreading rumors, posting embarrassing photographs, sending threatening e-mails, and making private e-mails public.

Sexual harassment and disrespect of women are also widespread problems on the Internet. Recent articles in the commercial press have described how cyberstalkers harass and threaten women (Nakashima, 2007). Kelly, Pomerantz, and Currie (2006) interviewed adolescent girls about their online experiences. Girls described how they tried to fight back against sexual harassment by displaying confidence and rebelling against stereotypical notions of femininity, but were unsuccessful in stopping masculine dominance.

Other studies show that the same stereotypical gender roles and relations that marginalize women in offline places are reproduced in online spaces. Thomas (2005) described how adolescent girls engaged in exaggerated behaviors of femininity online that interfered with online communications, like flirting and incessant giggling by using emoticons and chat language. Others (Subrahmanyam, Smahel, & Greenfield, 2006) found that older adolescent males engaged in crude language and explicit expressions of sexuality that offended girls in chat rooms. Flaming (insulting, name-calling, and using expletives) are other ways in which adolescent males marginalize and intimidate females in cyberspace (Guzzetti, 2008).

Finally, girls' contributions in online environments are often not acknowledged or elaborated on by others, particularly in male-dominated discussion groups. Girls' voices on message boards and electronic discussion lists can be silenced by being ignored. Lack of acknowledgment jeopardizes girls' participation, since females are less likely to persist in posting when their messages receive no response (Herring, 2001).

PROGRAMS THAT ADDRESS SOCIAL INJUSTICES IN DIY MEDIA

Many social service agencies, public information centers, private foundations, and government agencies have recognized these issues. These agencies attempt to address the racial, cultural, and gender inequities that create the digital divide through supplementary programs. Their intent is to help compensate for the limited access and capabilities of schools or homes or provide a supportive and safe environment for girls' participation in online communities.

After-School Programs

One of the largest types of programs that promote digital access are after-school and summer programs. Global Kids (www.globalkids.org) is an independent and nonprofit program based in low-performing New York City high schools, formed in collaboration with the New York City Department of Education, the After School Corporation, and the United Way of New York City. The mission of Global Kids is "to transform urban youth into successful students and global and community leaders by engaging them in socially dynamic content rich experiences." Through the virtual world of *Second Life*, Global Kids network with other students across the world to investigate and report on international issues. A machinima film, a computer animation done in a three-dimensional environment that some of these students created in the virtual world of Second Life, can be seen on the YouTube video (www. Youtube.com), *Global Kids Race to Equality*.

Gender Equity Programs

There are also after-school programs that specifically target either girls or boys to address gender inequities in technology. One of these after-school programs is CompuGirls (www.compugirls.asu.edu), a project that services adolescent girls from underresourced high schools in the Phoenix area in grades 8–12. This program, funded by the National Science Foundation (NSF), is conducted both after school and in summers and focuses on teaching participants digital skills as they investigate community issues of their choice, using the digital abilities and technologies they learn in the program to do so.

Perhaps the largest program that addresses gender injustice in digital literacies is the National Girls Collaborative Project (NGCP) (www.pugetsoundcenter.org/ngcp/). Funded by the National Science Foundation, this program provides resource sharing, conferences, a directory of girl-serving projects, and mini grants to girl-serving agencies to encourage young women in science, technology, engineering, and mathematics. Examples of these projects can be seen on YouTube.

Programs in Youth-Serving Agencies

Many youth-serving agencies also have programs to help to compensate for lack of access to digital technologies. These agencies also encourage youth in technology through their personnel who serve as role models. Youth workers in social service agencies are more likely than teachers to share racial, ethnic, and socioeconomic backgrounds and experiences and live in the same communities as the youth they serve (Rubinstein-Avilla, 2007).

These programs include projects by the Girl Scouts and the Boys and Girls Clubs. The Girl Scouts sponsors a Girls Go Tech program (www.girlsgotech.org)that provides computer workshops, a merit badge for achievement in digital technologies, a short film and video contest, and digital tools to create designs on the web. Their website contains descriptions of careers for girls in technology, a list of print and online resources, and a booklet of tips for parents to encourage and support girls in technology.

The Boys and Girls Clubs (BGCs) service youth ages 6 to 18, and are found in schools, public housing developments, homeless shelters, military bases, and on Native American lands. BGCs provide computer access and training with Club Tech. Club Tech provides fluency with the Internet, access to productivity software, such as word processing and spreadsheets, and offers creative and artistic software, such as digital arts and video editing (www.wikipedia.org/wiki/Boys_&_Girls_Clubs_of_America).

Community Technology Centers

Community Technology Centers (CTCs) offer resources to families to help bridge the digital divide by offering public access to computers and the Internet. Once funded by the U.S. Department of Education's Office of Vocational and Adult Education, these centers now rely on a variety of funding sources, including benefits, donations, other grant programs, and revenue-generating projects (www.Wikipedia.org/wiki/Community_technology_center). CTCs provide training in basic computer skills, digital media production, and applied computing skills. CTCs may be found in public libraries, schools, social service agencies, neighborhood centers, and religious centers.

Public Libraries

In 1993, public libraries began offering computer and Internet access to the public. Private foundations, such as the Gates Foundation, offer grants to help libraries improve the quality of their free computer access. These grants are needed because local libraries offer variable services. They often lack up-to-date computers with adequate bandwith for high-speed and reliable Internet access, and frequently have outdated programs (www.gathernodust.com/2008/05/public-access-computer-problem). Despite these problems, public libraries provide the only viable access to computers and the Internet for some students.

MOVING FORWARD: THE CHALLENGE OF DIY MEDIA

These outside resources are important not only because they provide access, but also because they provide the opportunity for teens to pursue their own interests and create their own media. Many adolescents perceive their use of computers in school to be boring and trivial (Gasmo, 2004). Yet young people engage in increasingly sophisticated digital literacy practices outside of school (Alvermann, 2002). Schools tend to play a minimal role in adolescents' learning of digital skills in comparison to their out-of-school learning, which is stimulated by popular culture, new media, and social networking (Kearney, 2006a). It is important to keep in mind that focusing solely on students' school-related literate abilities only in school itself suggests that young people have no life outside of school (Street, 1995). We believe that effective instruction is student–centered, acknowledges the complexity of the individual, and incorporates students' backgrounds and interests. By becoming familiar with and recognizing the importance of adolescents' DIY media, teachers can acknowledge their students as articulate and capable young people who have myriad ways of demonstrating their literate abilities.

CHAPTER 2

Blogs

Room12Space

Posts (RSS)   Comments (RSS)

home edit

18 September 2009
Efolio Technology post.

Posted by Mark Herring at 6:36 AM Labels: Efolio Tasks

Reactions: ☐ funny (0) ☐ Interesting (0) ☐ cool (0)

Here are the details of what to add to your efolio post about your Tri Team Product.

1. A description about what we did, how we did it and why?

2. An embed of the Matrix. (Tell the reader which group number you are)

3. A scanned and inserted image of your prototype drawing with labels. - What did you do to get some market research and change the prototype?

4. A photo of your finished product.

5. A photo and recount of you selling your product at our Market Day (You'll have to wait until after the market Day to do this...)

GREAT JOB! - now you could commment on someone elses post.

Search

About

This is the digital world of Learning Centre 12 at Riverdale School. Use this search bar to explore our site.

Google [   ] [Search]

Web - Images - News - Scholar - Go to Safe-Google.com

Safe Search uses Googles filtered SafeSearch technology. For more information please visit the Google SafeSearch help link.

The word "blog" is a shortened version of the term "we-blog." A blog is a platform through which an individual or a group can publish posts on a variety of subjects. These date-stamped entries are organized in reverse chronological order, with the newest post appearing at the top of the page. Blogs are often composed mainly of text content, although many include other media, such as videos, podcasts, audio files, or photos.

The universe of online blogging is called the *blogosphere*. By their nature, blogs are an online community. Sources disagree on exactly how many blogs there are, but Technorati, the first blog search engine, tracked 133 million blogs in 2008 (Technorati, 2008). Whatever the total may be, it is clear that blogs are so widespread that they have become mainstream (Helmond, 2008).

The blogosphere is vast and diverse. Some blogs may be personal and serve as an online diary; these blogs enjoy huge popularity among adolescents (Fox & Madden, 2006). Other blogs are used to share political commentary, reviews, or comments on society and culture. More recently, private companies, nonprofit organizations, and Hollywood movie stars have been using blogs to keep in touch with their customers, supporters, or fans.

The author of a blog is called a *blogger*, and many blogs are maintained solely by an individual blogger. Others are hosted by one or several blog editors, but contain contributions from a variety of bloggers. Readers can respond to a blog post in the form of a comment. Comments allow readers to leave their thoughts on, impressions of, and responses to a particular blog post.

Most blogs are open for public consumption, although blog-hosting sites (authoring services) often offer the ability to keep a post private so that only the user who authored it (or certain designated friends) can view it, which is referred to as "locking" it. A blog may be a hybrid of these levels of openness, with some posts viewable by everyone, other posts only viewable by friends, and still others that can be seen by no one but the blogger.

Blogs often contain both text and visuals. For example, photographs are commonly used to supplement a blog post, or as part of the background design of the blog. Bloggers may also include photos and links to other blogs, videos, news articles of interest, or other websites pertaining to the topic discussed in the blog. The blog format is very flexible, which has led to a diverse blogosphere.

BLOG-HOSTING SITES

LiveJournal (www.livejournal.com) was founded in 1999 and more than 16 million LiveJournals have been created since then. In a 2009 report on the Internet usage habits of college students over a 4-year period, LiveJournal was ranked the sixth most popular online site. LiveJournal was the only site of its kind that made it into the top 10 in this study (Anderson Analytics, 2008).

Blogger (www.blogger.com), another popular blog-hosting site, was also founded in 1999. This site is now owned by Google, but at least some of the site's original founders still work on Blogger as a team under the vast Google banner.

Tumblr (www.tumblr.com) is another blog-hosting platform that is quickly gaining popularity. It makes posting photos and other media simple. Tumblr is also known as a good tool for micro-blogging, or sharing short texts, photo, video, or audio clips rather than longer, more detailed posts. Another unique feature is the re-blog button on each Tumblr blog, which allows blogs to be disseminated broadly in much the same way as viral videos on YouTube.

Twitter is another popular micro-blogging tool through which users can send each other text-only updates, called "tweets," consisting of up to 140 characters. Users send tweets about life events, news stories of interest, links to websites, upcoming events, or any other piece of information. On Twitter, users are "followed" by other users who receive their tweets. Just like with Tumblr, tweets can be re-tweeted, which allows users to rapidly share short pieces of information with a wide audience.

WordPress (www.wordpress.org) is a blog-hosting site emphasizing catchy aesthetics and usability, resulting in a professional-looking blog. Founded in 2003, WordPress is an open-source project, which means that hundreds of people are working on it, making continuous improvements to enhance the experience of its users.

BLOGS AND TEENS

According to a study done in 2005 by the Pew Internet and American Life Project, 93% of all teens use the Internet and 19% of online teens keep a blog, making teens more likely than adults to have their own blog (Lenhart et al., 2007). The majority of these blogs are personal, serving as an open, online diary and a way to keep in touch with friends. Teens share information about themselves through blogs, including photographs, and thoughts about their schools, friends, relationships, pop culture events, and more. Teens who maintain their own blogs are far more likely to create other products on the Internet, including videos, drawings, and other self-made content, such as a personal web page, or a web page with a group of friends or one done for a class project (Lenhart & Madden, 2005).

Guzzetti and Gamboa (2005a) investigated how two adolescent girls used LiveJournal; their findings illustrated the range of ways that teens use blogs. The young women in their study blurred the boundaries between school and home literacies by writing in their LiveJournals both in and out of school and by linking their online journals to classroom instruction. One girl copied her notes from her social studies class into her journal and used LiveJournal to practice her German by blogging to her boyfriend in the language. Another wrote about her desire to create a children's story about nontraditional families that reflected what she had learned in her Women's Studies class and to express herself by including her philosophies about feminism and the war in Iraq.

BLOG SAFETY AND PRIVACY

Many personal blogs contain embarrassing or inflammatory posts that later may cause regret. Blogs are not always permanent because many blog-hosting sites delete them after a period of inactivity, but content from abandoned blogs may still be available through web archives years after the blogger has discontinued posting. This is a concern for adolescents who may feel comfortable writing openly about something, but regret it when they are older and have different viewpoints, wish to be more private, or find that they have posted material that could prevent them from getting into college or being hired for a job. It is always a good idea for bloggers to carefully consider what they share online, and whether they will still feel comfortable with sharing that information years later.

Information on blog safety, particularly for teens, is readily available on the web. The community WiredSafety (www.wired safety.org) is an especially helpful tool that offers tips for teens and parents to blog safely.

TYPES OF BLOGS

Blogs for Social Good

Nonprofit organizations and political organizers use blogs to keep in touch with supporters of their causes. Many of these blogs have so many fans and enjoy so much widespread support that they have created an impassioned online community of activists and supporters. Blogs are an online way for these groups to promote offline activities. The Planned Parenthood Federation of America operates a blog, I Am Emily X (www.iamemilyx.blogspot.com) to post videos and calls to action in support of pro-choice issues.

Some blogs for social good may not be overtly political in nature, but rather serve as a platform to raise social consciousness about a specific issue. One example is the art blog PostSecret (www.post secret.blogspot.com). PostSecret is hosted on the popular hosting site Blogger and features new content each Sunday. PostSecret is an ongoing community art and writing project in which people send in their secrets anonymously on a postcard. Individuals can create art on one side of a postcard, and then write a secret on the other side. The blog editor, Frank Warren, started PostSecret in January 2005, and since that time has published the artwork of thousands of people who mail him their deepest secrets. PostSecret offers a community for adolescents to share their feelings without fear of judgment and is hugely popular among adolescents.

Blogs for Political Commentary

Political blogs focus on tracking news stories and analyzing the political world. Most blogs have an obvious ideological leaning, ranging across the political spectrum. Readers count on blogs to provide greater detail and commentary on current news stories. In addition, political blogs offer a place for political enthusiasts to discuss news stories of interest and express their worldviews and political perspectives.

The Huffington Post, an online newspaper, offers a multitude of blogs through which many commentators offer their thoughts on news, politics, and culture. As is typical of many large blogs with multiple bloggers, a user can access blog posts alphabetically by author, or in descending order of blogs that have been viewed the most, have the most reader comments, or have been e-mailed the most. Readers can also narrow their reading to bloggers they especially enjoy and comment only on those posts.

Blogs for Celebrity Gossip

As passionate about politics as some bloggers are, there are also many blogs devoted to detailing the personal lives of celebrities. These blogs include everything from rumors of romantic relationships to photos of television and movie actors eating lunch or walking down the street. They are immensely popular among teens. Perez Hilton is among the web's most famous gossip blogger, known for his uncensored coverage of celebrity gossip. He is famous for posting tabloid photos doctored with his own crude captions (www.perezhilton.com.). Hilton's ascension into notoriety in the offline world is a nod to the enormous popularly and potential of celebrity gossip blogs.

BLOGS IN CLASSROOMS

Many educators are already using blogs to engage their students. Blogs can be created for free on platforms such as Blogger or www.edublogs.org. Teachers can use a classroom blog to track assignments and allow students to respond to questions via the comment feature. A classroom blog can be an efficient way to keep track of students' learning over a semester or academic year.

By posting to a blog each day or at the end of each lesson, students create a record of their time together and can create new content based on what they learned. Students can use the class blog for an aggregate look at what they have done in each class. Students could also use a class blog to review for a final exam. Blogs can be used in any subject area to discuss and articulate concepts or skills in both a personalized and group exchange and to build on previous content concepts or topics (Huffaker, 2005). Blogs can host art, photos, and videos along with or in place of text content. They can be a place to post links for further readings, to survey the class, to ask questions about reading assignments, or to extend and continue in-class discussions.

This ability to incorporate various media is an innovative way to teach to a variety of learning styles. Students who have trouble with traditional methods of learning may be more successful learning via media like blogs that they can relate to and are already comfortable using. For example, visual learners can watch videos and auditory learners could listen to a podcast of the same content.

Keeping a classroom blog also allows for extended learning outside of school and the ability for parents to cross-check students' learning. Parents may use a class blog to review what their student is learning at school so those lessons can be followed up at home. Students who are absent from class could use a class blog to catch up on assignments and communicate with other students. A class blog allows access to the community established within a classroom anywhere there is an Internet connection.

Limitations to Using Blogs in the Classroom

Despite these benefits, there are several caveats teachers will need to be aware of in using blogs in classrooms. Teachers will need to use caution when assigning students to create a blog for free-choice writing assignments. Topics that are acceptable in the blogosphere may not be appropriate subject matter for classroom assignments. Teens tend to share personal information on blogs that should not be shared in a classroom, so they may have to be reminded of the need to write only about school-appropriate topics. Students will need to be cautioned that cyberbullying will not be tolerated.

Finally, using blogs in the classroom may present issues about the appropriate use of formal versus informal writing style. Teens are notorious for using the shorthand language of text messaging or "cyberspeak" in their writing online. A student may write, "Rulz abt writing need 2 b clear" when she means "Rules about writing need to be clear." Cyberspeak is showing up in students' writing assignments in school, so teachers may need to discuss with their students what type of writing is school-appropriate and what type is inappropriate.

Examples of Class Blogs

Many teachers have experimented with using classroom blogs, some with much success (for tips, visit: http://www.edutopia.org/student.blogging-classroomtips). One example comes from an English teacher, Jessie Thaler, who used a blog with her eighth-grade students (thalerscholars.blogspot.com). She encouraged her students to use Blogger for their writing assignments. Her students began by writing poetry, and then progressed to journal entries, and eventually blogged longer writings. A chemistry teacher used a blog to facilitate her students' writing about forensic concepts (Guzzetti, in press). At the end of the unit, she invited her students to write murder mysteries and post them on a class blog created by her school district, read the stories, peer-edit, and review them. She held a contest to determine which story used the most forensic clues and forensic science procedures and declared a winner in each class. Students enjoyed reading one another's forensic mysteries, and wrote words of encouragement and praise for their classmates' stories.

Support for Using Blogs in Teaching

Several organizations encourage using technology in the classroom and offer useful resources for teachers looking for ideas or a community of other teachers with whom to share ideas. One such organization is the eMints National Center (www.emints.org). The eMints National Center offers information on incorporating blogs, wikis, and other technology into the classroom. Edutopia (www.edutopia.org), created by the George Lucas Educational Foundation, offers resources, encouragement, and advice to educators who want to immerse their students in technology-focused education. A particularly helpful blog devoted to information about and dialogue on implementing blogs in the classroom is available at www.weblogg-ed.com.

LITERACY SKILLS AND ABILITIES IN BLOGGING

There are numerous traditional and new literacy skills and abilities fostered by blogging. Perhaps one of the most prevalent is the ability to write for a specific audience—peers—and writing for a purpose—writing for self-expression and identity representation. Bloggers are typically writing for their friends for social reasons. Blogging enhances students' writing abilities in the genre of storytelling (Penrod, 2007).

In blogging, students learn to read and write in hybrid forms by incorporating graphics and texts, and see writing as a visual enterprise (Penrod, 2007). They enhance their verbal literacies of reading and writing, as well as their digital fluency with technology, by using features such as hyperlinks. They learn the digital literacy skills required to read and write in online forums, and when reading one another's blogs and responding, students think and read critically by sorting and evaluating the information they are receiving (Penrod, 2007).

Suggestions for Teaching in Content Areas with Blogs

- English/language arts teachers can use blogs for developing students' story-writing abilities by peer critique and editing of classmates' story elements, such as plot, theme, and character development.
- Science teachers can ask individuals to use a blog to predict the results of an experiment and later debrief by discussing their results of the experiment and the scientific principles it illustrated.
- Mathematics teachers can have their students record in their blogs how they applied mathematical principles in word problems.
- Social studies teachers might ask students to take a position on a historical figure or issue in their blogs and discuss pros and cons of a famous figure's contributions or particular political issues.

CHAPTER 3

Social Networking and Social Media Sites

*S*ocial networking and *social media* are terms used to describe web services such as MySpace, Facebook, and Twitter. *Social networking* refers to the connection of users to other users through personal friendship networks, school and work groups, and online communities. These platforms are used to keep in touch with friends near and far, engage with people who have similar interests, and share ideas and emotions with an online community. These frameworks offer users the ability to communicate with hundreds, even thousands, of other users with just a few clicks.

Social media is another term used to describe these applications. Social media refers to sharing and discussing information with a large group of people. For example, on Facebook a user can share a video he or she created that blasts (or sends) the video to their friends' pages and allows for discussion of the video. Friends can forward the video to their social networks; this is how amateur videos gain such an impressive audience.

Many platforms exhibit qualities of both social networking and social media, and often the distinction really rests in how the platforms are used. Either can be used to connect with people (social networking) or share information (social media). Both aspects are important to DIY media. Although these tools are not used to create DIY media, they are essential vehicles to share user-created content such as videos, photos, writing, and music. We refer to these tools and platforms as social networking throughout this chapter, although in most cases they are also used for social media purposes.

TEENS AND SOCIAL NETWORKING

Multiple functions of sites such as Facebook, MySpace, and Twitter mean that these platforms can be considered social networking, social media, and micro-blogging tools. Whatever the term, they are very popular with adolescents. About 50% of teens in the United States use MySpace, Facebook, or another social networking site at least once a day (Lenhart & Fox, 2006).

Youth use these sites in ways that have transformed how they form relationships, build complex communities, share ideas, and discover and use new information (Lewis, Leander, & Wang, 2007). For example, within 24 hours following the shooting of 33 people at Virginia Tech, Facebook groups were created by students at the school and at other colleges across the country (Wilbur, 2008). Students from all over the world displayed a black ribbon graphic along with words of comfort, poetry, and prayers, urging others to reach out to loners (Heffernan, 2007). International students coming to the United States use social networking sites such as MySpace to keep in touch with friends and families back home. Teens in other countries such as Brazil, Argentina, and Chile use social networking sites at Internet cafes to document their lives (Rubinstein-Avilla, 2009).

Teens' use of these sites indicates the local and global nature of the Net Generation's digital literacy practices that allow them to publish and communicate on the global stage (Schultz, Vasudevan, & Throop, 2007). Sites such as MySpace signal changing patterns in adolescents' purposes for and use of literacies (Alvermann, 2002). These texts are artifacts that illustrate shifts toward global citizenship (Schultz, Vasudevan, & Throop, 2007).

COMMON FEATURES OF SOCIAL NETWORKING SITES

There are some features common to social networking sites that promote and enhance their DIY aspects. Each site requires a user to create a user name and a password. Some people use their names, while other users may choose a nickname.

Friends

Without online "friends," social networking platforms would be pointless. Friends are other users accepted into the user's social network. Friends may be people whom the user knows in real life, or people with similar interests whom the user does not know outside of the online social network. The value of this tool is the ability to build online social networks and share information.

Applications

Facebook and MySpace have also created platforms for software developers to create applications that can be used by their users. Thousands of applications have appeared on Facebook and were introduced later on MySpace, but are not as numerous there. Facebook applications include Gifts, through which users send virtual gifts to one another; Events, which allows users to create a virtual invitation, invite other users, and a mechanism for invitees to RSVP; and Quizzes designed by users meant to be taken by friends to see how well they know each other.

Comments and Messages

Comments are an important function on MySpace and Facebook. On Facebook, comments are posted to the user's "Wall" and then integrated into the user's profile. The Wall captures interactions between the user and his or her friends. Facebook allows users to comment on every aspect of a user's profile, including photos, application notices, and status updates.

Comments are not the only way that users can communicate, but are a popular form of interaction within social networking platforms. Often, comments are viewable not only by the user to whom the comment was directed, but also by anyone who has access to that user's profile. If one user wants to send something to another user privately, that person uses the messaging feature available on both MySpace and Facebook. Messages allow users to communicate back and forth. Users can embed photos, links, and other items.

Photos and Videos

Photos are a popular feature on both MySpace and Facebook. Photos can be organized into albums that allow other users to view them and comment on each photo or an album in its entirety. Users can "tag" other users in photos on both MySpace and Facebook. After a user is tagged, the photo will appear with the tagged user's photos. Videos that adolescents find or create can be recorded by using a webcam or other camcorder and uploaded to both MySpace and Facebook, which is how amateur videos published on YouTube and other video sites gain widespread popularity.

CONCERNS ABOUT SOCIAL NETWORKING SITES

Teachers and administrators share hesitations about using social networking sites in middle and high schools. There are some general concerns that should be considered in the debate.

Time Management

Many adults and teens debate about whether social networking sites enhance human communication and access to information or are a distraction from important learning and useful communication. For some parents, teachers, and administrators, social networking may represent time spent distracted from rather than engaged in relevant learning and communication. Hence, social networking sites like MySpace and Facebook may not be the best tools to incorporate into schools.

Privacy

Privacy is both a philosophical and practical concern with the social networking phenomenon. Critics are concerned about chronic oversharing of personal information. Social networking has been called narcissistic, and some worry that social networking is contributing to the "dumbing down" of America.

More practically, privacy is a real concern. Employers and schools are investigating applicants via their social networking accounts, and many also monitor employees' use of these tools both in and outside the workplace or school. Adolescents should be concerned not only about their employers checking their sites, but also that child predators use social networking sites to prey on teens. Stalkers also use social networking sites to track victims.

Cyberbullying

Social networking sites are popular forums for cyberbullying. Teens use social networking sites to taunt and harass their peers by posting negative remarks, calling names, jeering, or making sexual innuendos. For some teens, social networking may be a crucial part of their social lives offline, which may be impacted by online harassment. Online harassment can be just as painful and humiliating as offline harassment and can go unnoticed by adults.

HELPING TEENS PROTECT THEMSELVES

There are several tactics that teens can take to protect themselves online. Many users make their social networking accounts viewable by friends only, and only accept Friend Requests from people they know outside the online community. Some users do not use their real names, and many are careful to leave out identifying information, like an address or phone number.

Teens need to be especially cautious about what they post on the Internet. Safe Internet practices should be shared with adolescents, who can be naïve regarding the need for Internet safety. The following are some questions that could be posed to preteens and teens to help them think critically about their Internet use:

- Do you post anything you would not want a specific person in your life to see, such as a parent, teacher, current or future employer, friend, family member, or college admissions staff?
- Do you give out identifying information like an address or phone number? Do you post your school, your daily schedule, or your place of employment?
- Do you communicate with people on social networking sites whom you have never met in real life? How do you know what these people tell you is true?

Regardless of whether social networking is merely permitted or actively encouraged in school, it is important for teachers to be aware of these concerns and share them with teens.

LITERACY SKILLS AND SOCIAL NETWORKING SITES

Reading and writing on social networking sites give adolescents new purposes for and practice with writing. These include building social networks, establishing new relationships, forming complex communities, discovering and using new information, and sharing ideas and opinions (Lewis, Leander, & Wang, 2008). Through their interactions on social networking sites, students learn a variety of digital literacies. They learn how to copy and paste HTML code to modify their MySpace and Facebook pages (Wilbur, 2008). They write in hybrid textual forms, and think carefully about the inclusion and interaction of a variety of multimedia elements in their writing. These elements include photos, color, sound, hyperlinks, symbols, graphics, and descriptions of self (Wilbur, 2008). Young people learn writing as a multimodal art that involves intertextuality, or referring to and linking to other texts, and make use of multimodal texts. Reading and writing on social networking sites such as MySpace and Facebook are "very detailed endeavors in which every little bit counts against the whole and attention to detail pays off in the end" (Wilbur, 2008, p. 66).

USING SOCIAL NETWORKING SITES IN CLASSROOMS

There are appropriate ways to take the concepts of social networking and social media and apply them in the classroom. Teachers will need to think carefully about how to construct a limited, closed network that will bring students together online and allow them to share information in an innovative yet familiar way. Many educators have already explored appropriate ways that these concepts can be applied for classroom use and have found substitutes for platforms like MySpace and Facebook.

The use of a closed, managed online environment with a teacher as the administrator is probably the best way to incorporate social networking concepts in schools. With a managed environment, an educator can restrict the social network to a particular group (just students; students and teachers; or students, teachers, and parents are example groups), decide which applications will be used, screen content before it can be viewed by all users, or delete inappropriate content. A managed environment keeps the focus on school use, and students should be able to separate this school-based platform from their other social networking habits.

Free Social Networking Sites for Classrooms

A platform to create an online managed environment tool can be found in ELGG (www.elgg.com), which offers customized social networking platforms based on an organization's needs. This company offers a selection of the basic tools found on MySpace and Facebook, but with the additional ability of a controlled online environment. Platforms like this one are viable alternatives to more public online spaces.

Ning (www.ning.com) is another free tool that teachers can use to create a closed and managed online social network. Ning competes with larger social sites such as MySpace and Facebook by allowing users to create their own social networks around specific interests (Lidetke, 2007). In a matter of minutes, teachers can sign up for a Ning account and create their own customizable social network.

This social network can be open to the public so that parents can join or closed to the public so that other users such as students in a particular classroom could join by invitation only. Ning offers users customizability in format and features as well, such as allowing users to create their own visual design, choice of features, and member data. A teacher could enlist the help of class members in designing the network and ultimately be in charge of administering that network.

Support for Using Online Social Networking in Teaching

Creation and administration of an online social network may be a challenge for teachers at the outset. Teachers will need to be comfortable enough with technology to outline the specific purposes for the social network, motivate students to take part, and perform ongoing maintenance and control of the site. The power to network students to one another and share information in a new and stimulating way can yield exciting results. That is why some teachers are already implementing social networking and other Web 2.0 tools in their classrooms.

Aside from social networking in the classroom, teachers may find a social network with other educators helpful. Many of these networks already exist and provide educators with a space to discuss using technological innovations in the classroom. The Schools United (www.theschoolsunited.com) is the first site dedicated to social networking in education. Classroom 2.0 (www.classroom20.com) is a place for teachers to collaborate and is an example of the power of online social networks. It was created using Ning and includes tips on building and using a Ning network for student-based social networking. Classroom 2.0 partners with PBS Teachers to offer a series of free monthly webinars (seminars, lectures, and workshops broadcast over the web) for pre-K–12 educators to learn new ways to integrate online instructional resources into their teaching.

Suggestions for Teaching in Content Areas

- Social studies teachers could have students set up a Ning account by acting as particular historical figures or politicians; each student could represent a figure and post comments from that figure's point of view.
- English teachers could have students create a Ning account by assuming the identity of an author they are currently studying and write sentences that reflect the author's writing style, and critique or extend them.
- Art teachers could have students create a Ning or Flickr account that contains photos, color, and collage and have their class members contribute their own designs and comment on their peers' work.

- English/language arts teachers could have students keep a Facebook profile for the protagonist from a book they are reading. They could write status updates documenting significant events of the story, maintaining a voice appropriate for the age and personality of the character.
- Social studies teachers could assign students to create a Facebook profile belonging to a historical figure from any time period, complete with images and descriptions of where they are and what they are doing at the time, and include quotes, favorite things, and groups that the person might join.
- Teachers in any content area could maintain a Flickr account for photos of class projects and events. Parents could view them as a way to be informed about students' assignments.

CHAPTER 4

Video Games, Machinima, and Virtual Worlds

During the past few decades, video games have become a huge part of youth culture. Adolescents engage in a wide range of video games, including first-person shooters, simulation games, and fantasy, adventure, and mystery games. According to a national survey, about half of all teens (Lenhart, Kahne, et al., 2008) and about 70% of college students play video games (Jones, 2003).

ADOLESCENTS CREATING VIDEO GAMES

Many adolescents who are avid fans of gaming modify commercial video games or create their own. Many commercial video games have software built into them by the publishers that enables players to change the game or create their own modifications that extend the original game. For example, *Civilization* has built-in tools that allow players to create new "maps" of the world. Publishers encourage video gamers to change parts or all of a game by altering its code and supplying its source code and the tools to alter it. These tools usually consist of a game engine (the core software system on which the game runs) and "modding tools" (graphic editors and software code libraries) that allow modifications to the original game (Hayes & Games, 2008). Manufacturers of these games have discovered that supplying this software extends the shelf life of video games and helps to build community (Hyman, 2004).

The process of modifying games is called "modding." "Modders" may change the difficulty level, the style of play, the avatars or characters' appearance, or the rules. Or they may change the entire game. An example of a popular modded game is *Counter-Strike*, which is based on a mod of the game *Half-Life* created by players from the developers' software. Creating new material for existing games or modding games is often a step toward designing new games and facilitates learning design skills (Hayes & Games, 2008).

There are also computer software programs for purchase that allow users to invent games, such as *Stagecast* (www.stagecast.com). *Stagecast* has tutorials with modding tools that enable players to create their own two-dimensional video games. Some players who do not purchase this software may hack into the software of commercial games that do not provide modding tools and pirate their software. While many hackers in fact create their own new video games, piracy is a practice that is illegal, and one that we do not advocate. However they are created, student-made video games can be just as well crafted or better than commercial games (Gee, 2003).

CRITICISMS OF VIDEO GAMES

Many educators have derided video games as mindless entertainment and a waste of time. Games are considered amusements that encourage violence offline (Sanders, 1995) and promote a culture of instant gratification and aggression (Anderson, 2003). Some critics have claimed that electronic activities like video games are responsible for a lack of engagement in literacy (Weber, 2004).

EDUCATIONAL BENEFITS OF PLAYING VIDEO GAMES

Proponents of video games counter that they do not replace literacy activities, but are in themselves literacy activities (e.g., Gee, 2003; Steinkuehler, 2007). Video games can teach children thinking and reading skills, particularly those new literacy skills and abilities that will be increasingly needed for the 21st century (Johnson, 2005; Kafai, 1995). Even games that aren't overtly educational teach "soft skills," such as critical thinking, problem solving, prioritizing, and decision making (Gee, 2003). Unlike sports or board games where participants must know the rules and how to exploit them before they begin playing, it's common for video games to start players with a few basic directions and leave it up to them to figure out what to do next. Players must pay close attention to their environment to progress in a video game (Johnson, 2005).

Playing video games may also enhance students' motor skills. There is evidence that playing video games increases hand–eye coordination. Surgeons who spent at least three hours a week playing video games made about 37% fewer mistakes in laparoscopic surgery than did their peers who did not play video games (Dobner, 2004). Others have reported that producing video games improves students' spatial skills (Cassell & Jenkins, 1998).

EDUCATIONAL BENEFITS OF CREATING VIDEO GAMES

Most importantly, in playing and creating video games young people develop a sophisticated design mind-set that allows them to think about video games as designed objects (Gee, 2003). This creative, problem-solving mentality has been recognized by scholars to be a fundamental ability required for full participation in the knowledge economy (e.g., Gee, Hull, & Lankshear, 1996). Employers hire workers who can produce new knowledge that can help their companies adapt and become competitive in the global market (Nussbaum, 2005).

Design Thinking

Design thinking is a way of thinking about solving problems and creating a strategy by experimenting. Design thinking is increasingly being required by business leaders who want their employees to identify creative solutions to complex challenges (Hyer, 2006). Design thinking involves working collaboratively in teams, testing new ideas, prototyping and failing, reflecting on failures, and making changes (Hyer, 2006), all of which are fostered by creating video games.

Operational Literacies

Video games also require operational literacies, including competence with the tools, procedures, and techniques involved in understanding the written language system of games (Lankshear & Knobel, 2003). These skills include being able to read, write, and key in code in a range of contexts. Sanford and Madill (2007) found that game designers understand the ways in which computers work, use visual and written tutorials, apply procedures to craft stages of their games, test out their applications by playing the game, and apply their past computer experiences to new situations.

Cultural Literacies

Adolescents who create video games also develop cultural literacies (Sanford & Madill, 2007), or knowing how to make and grasp meanings appropriately within a given practice (Green, 1997). This implies knowing what a practice like video gaming is about and the context of the practice, which dictates appropriate or inappropriate ways of reading and writing within that practice (Lankshear & Knobel, 2003). Sanford and Madill saw students enacting cultural literacies in creating video games like asking their peers for help, asking peers to try out their games, critiquing their peers' games, giving suggestions for making games better, using narrative characterization and themes, and thinking about their peers as their audience.

Technological Literacies

Technological literacies are those skills and abilities that allow gamers to model and learn for themselves by exploring new technologies, and to experiment and try out new aspects of hardware and software (Sanford & Madill, 2007). These include importing visual and print texts; gamers learn programming concepts and how to create rules for movement and interaction. They also learn how to incorporate elements of play and story into their games.

Traditional Literacies

In addition to developing these new literate abilities, adolescents who create video games enhance their traditional literacy skills (Sanford & Madill, 2007). Boys who created video games showed evidence of using literary devices, such as symbolism and contrast, in game creation. They developed and reinforced their vocabulary, particularly computer and video game terminology, and used unfamiliar words in meaningful contexts.

GENDER DISPARITIES IN LITERACY AND GAMING

Traditionally, boys have been considered literacy outsiders who more often than girls have lacked traditional literacy skills and abilities (Skelton, 2001). But video games have attracted males more than females. Gee (2003) reports that "boys are resisting school literacies where they have repeatedly been unsuccessful and instead are becoming literate in the semiotic domain of gaming which opens experiences in different ways of speaking, listening, viewing, and representing" (p. 18). Video games are spaces where boys have been successful (Sanford & Madill, 2007).

Educational researchers recognize that boys are now gaining at a greater rate than girls the new literacy skills and abilities and the mind-set of design thinking that will be increasingly needed in the 21st-century workforce. Women enroll in computer science courses in much smaller numbers than men (Dean, 2007). Video games that might induct them into technology fields are usually not designed for or marketed to girls (Denner, Werner, Bean, & Campe, 2005).

As a result of this gender disparity, the National Science Foundation funds educational projects to support females in technology. One of these is Girls Creating Games (GCG), a program for middle school girls. Girls create video games with Macromedia's Flash program of interactive story narratives in which players select a path at key points in the story to create their own events. The program stresses learning by design, scaffolding, modeling, collaborative learning, and identity formation (Denner, Werner, Bean, & Campe, 2007).

Educators can also address gender disparity through fostering critical perspectives on game consumption and production. Overrepresentation of male characters, female subordination, and violence are features of video games like *Grand Theft Auto* that repel females' participation. Therefore, like Sanford and Madill (2007), we encourage teachers to critically engage students with video games by considering ways to express gender equity when consuming or creating them.

CREATING VIDEO GAMES IN CONTENT AREAS

Students have made their own video games in mathematics, social studies, and language arts. Students in elementary schools, middle schools, and high schools have created their own video games to reinforce content concepts. Researchers have focused on how students' thinking shifts when they move from consumer/player to producer/creator and have documented how this shift in thinking impacted their learning of content concepts (e.g., Sanford & Madill, 2007).

One of the first projects that focused on making games to foster mathematical thinking was done with fourth graders (Kafai, 1995). Students produced video games to teach fractions to younger students. The students who created games performed better than those who did not on measures of fraction knowledge.

The *Civilization* games, about the growth and development of world civilizations, are popular with social studies teachers because they incorporate historical facts and concepts in the curriculum. Students used *Civilization III* to enact historically accurate scenarios and used modding tools to create colonial simulations (Squire, Giovanetto, Devane, & Durga, 2005). The game helped students make accurate observations and interpretations about history and form relevant questions about historical events.

A third project used the *Neverwinter Nights* role-playing game and a researcher-constructed platform, *AdventureAuthor* to foster children's literacy skills and storytelling through game design (Robertson & Good, 2004). Students created original storylines in video game form by using the Aurora toolset to modify the environments, characters, and story of the game, and used *AdventureAuthor* to design their games. Learners engaged in exploratory play, idea generation, design implementation, evaluation, and testing.

Support for Creating Video Games in the Classroom

Those who want to try making video games with students may be helped by accessing commercial software. One example is the aforementioned *Stagecast*, which lets kids develop simple games without learning programming skills. Creating a game in *Stagecast* involves using characters that can be edited and animated to interact with one another and their surroundings. *Stagecast* is easy to learn, and even children between 7 and 11 years old have been able to create games with *Stagecast* (Habgood, Ainsworth, & Benford, 2005). Tutorials and sample lessons are accessible through *Stagecast*'s website (www.stagecast.com/school).

Game Maker (www.yoyogames.com/gamemaker) is a programming tool to facilitate creating 2D and 3D games. Its interface follows the Microsoft Windows design style and allows users to make games by defining objects, like rooms (game screens), backgrounds, sprites (animated characters or objects), and sounds that can be customized by users. Basic games can be developed in *Game Maker* through a point-and-click interface. Tutorials, scripting language, and a textbook are available.

VIRTUAL WORLDS

A virtual world is an interactive, simulated environment accessed by multiple users through an online interface (www.virtualworlds areview.com/info/whatis). Virtual worlds differ from video games in that they are not limited to gaming, but can simulate the offline worlds of their users. Virtual worlds can be used for education, commerce, and socializing, and are characterized by user-generated content that makes their DIY aspects extensive.

Virtual worlds are shared spaces that allow many users to participate at once. They have graphical user interfaces in three-dimensional environments in which interactions take place in real time. Virtual worlds allow users to alter, develop, or build content and encourage the formation of in-world social groups.

There are more than 60 virtual worlds, including *Cyworld*, *Habbo Hotel*, *Twinity*, *Whyville*, *Active Worlds*, and *Second Life*. The most popular of these is *Second Life* (SL), a three-dimensional virtual world created by its residents, and its counterpart, *Teen Second Life* (TSL), for adolescents ages 13 through 17. In SL and TSL, residents communicate by instant messaging, text chatting, or voice communications as they navigate, consume, and construct. Residents travel, explore, socialize, create, learn, and trade virtual property and services. Although there are premium memberships that allow residents to build and sell property, a basic membership is free of charge, and there are many free goods and services that residents provide to one another.

Educational Projects in Virtual Worlds

There are several educational projects based in the virtual world of *Teen Second Life*. Perhaps the best known of these is Global Kids (www.globalkids.org), based in New York City high schools. Global Kids research international social issues by networking with other adolescents globally via TSL. These students develop digital literacies, including building, scripting, and making machinima (films made from video game software) in the virtual world that have real-world relevance. Examples of their projects can be found on YouTube (www.YouTube.com) videos. These include *Global Kids Race to Equality: A Second Life Machinima*, in which teens were enabled through their avatars and TSL surroundings to story their "first-life" experiences facing racial prejudice while growing up as children of color.

MACHINIMA

Pronounced ma-SHIN-uh-muh, machinima is a *portmanteau* of the words "machine" and "cinema." In the words of the Academy of Machinima Arts and Sciences, machinima is "real-world filmmaking techniques applied within an interactive virtual space, often using 3D video-game technologies" (http://www.machinima.org/machinima-faq.html). Machinima creators, sometimes called "machinimists" or "machinimators," create their videos by manipulating the visuals from video games, a process called "digital puppetry," and recording by using a video camera or screen-capture software, such as Fraps (www.fraps.com) or CamStudio (camstudio. org). They transfer video data to a computer, where they edit it with video editing software and add their own soundtrack, music, and voice-overs. The final products are shared on websites such as Machinima.com or YouTube. The most popular video games used to create machinima are *World of Warcraft*, *Half-Life*, *Halo*, *Call of Duty*, and the virtual worlds of *Second Life* and *Teen Second Life*. Some newer console games also have features manufactured into the game that facilitate producing machinima.

"Sprite movies" can also be considered a form of machinima. A "sprite" is an animation of a character, object, or scenery from a video game. These images can be found on the Internet as "sprite sheets," or pages that show every image used to make up the animation, and are animated with the Flash animation program on top of a background, either original or captured from a video game, and enhanced with music, sound effects, and voice-overs.

LITERACY SKILLS AND ABILITIES IN VIDEO GAMING

Consuming and producing video games and using virtual worlds exemplifies how thinking, reading, and writing are changing (Wilbur, 2008). Video games and virtual worlds are multimodal texts that require particular modalities of oral or written language, images, graphs, or symbols to communicate (Gee, 2003). Individuals must make generalizations, draw conclusions, understand complex vocabulary, and analyze and evaluate content (Salinger, 2007). Video games give students opportunities to practice these literacy skills in virtual spaces (Rhodes & Robnolt, 2009).

Players of video games and residents of virtual worlds learn new digital literacies. They must learn to read and interpret multiple and simultaneous information on the screen. They read and write in a hybrid text containing abbreviations, specialized vocabulary, truncations, typographical errors, grammatical errors, and syntactic erosions (Black & Steinkuehler, 2009). They learn to take critical perspectives, move among sign systems to gain new perspectives, and produce knowledge in collaborative ways (Leland, Harste, & Kuonen, 2008). Video games and virtual worlds give users new purposes for reading and writing. Video game players read the screen to track action, keep score, communicate with other players, and advance the game (Wilbur, 2008).

USING VIDEO GAMES
AND VIRTUAL WORLDS IN CLASSROOMS

Video games can be used in classrooms in two approaches—instructivism and constructivism (Kafai, 2006). The most popular approach is instructivism, or the use of educational games in school or after-school programs. This approach is based on the belief that video games are more motivating than traditional classroom activities (Hayes & Games, 2008), and includes the use of commercial games.

The second approach is constructivism, or engaging students in making their own games. This approach requires providing learners with game development tools, such as authoring software, and support for learning to use the tools. Players move from passive consumer/player roles to more active roles of producers and creators (Sanford & Madill, 2007). Creating video games allows students to learn programming skills, collaborate with others, become a member of a community, and develop their capacities for sustained engagement (Peppler & Kafai, 2007b).

Suggestions for Teaching with Video Games and Virtual Worlds

Rather than dismissing students' interest in gaming as counterproductive to learning, teachers can recognize that students learn valuable literacy skills from gaming, and that video games and virtual worlds can get students excited about subject matter. We offer the following suggestions for teaching:

- English/Language Arts and art teachers might have students create three-dimensional sculptures of their avatar and write their rationales for creating their avatar's appearance, including their names, ethnicities, genders, body type, hair, and fashion style.
- Math teachers when teaching graphing might use 8-bit pixel art, which is an arrangement of squares on a matrix, to give students an introduction to graphing.
- English/Language Arts teachers might use the intriguing characters and narratives from video games to initiate discussion of narrative features across different media.
- Business and social studies teachers might use the computer game *SimCity* as a way to help students

understand concepts in social studies and civics. Players design and nurture a city (of which they are the "mayor"), and learn about zoning, tax rates, public services, utilities, and more.

- Physics teachers might use video games like *Crayon Physics*, in which players get to see what their drawings would look like if converted to real objects, and *World of Goo*, a physics-based puzzle game, as a springboard to discussing physics concepts and a basis to create new physics games along these lines.
- Math teachers could use *Second Life* building tools to teach geometric concepts, including relationships among x, y, and z axes.

CHAPTER 5

YouTube and Video Sharing Sites

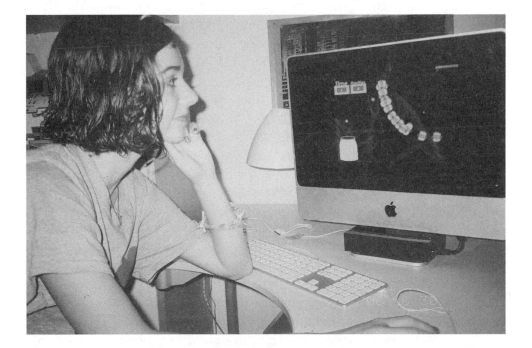

Almost any teenager who uses the Internet for entertainment has watched a video on YouTube or a similar video sharing website. Young people use these sites to post, share, and view homemade videos or watch professional music videos and clips from TV shows, movies, and online series. Some videos are so popular that they are called "viral videos," named for the viruslike rate at which they are spread among Internet users through e-mail and word of mouth. Video producing and online sharing have become an important part of Internet culture.

YOUTUBE: BROADCAST YOURSELF

Founded in February 2005 and now owned by Google, YouTube is the most commonly used platform for individuals to post videos. YouTube is also the most popular site for online video sharing among teens, who, according to the Nielson Company, typically watch 11 minutes of online videos a day (Szalai & Uni, 2009). The typical teen spends 3 hours a month engaged with online videos, mostly through YouTube.

YouTube facilitates video sharing with an easy-to-use interface that uses Adobe Flash video technology to allow millions to watch a video that was created in just a few minutes. YouTube videos can be integrated with social networking sites like Facebook or MySpace through a process called "embedding." Videos can also be embedded in other web pages or blogs or viewed on mobile phones. YouTube videos can be posted publicly so that anyone can view them or privately so that the video can only be viewed by the user and/or the user's YouTube friends.

WHY IS YOUTUBE SO POPULAR?

There are several reasons for YouTube's explosive popularity. One reason is the interactive quality that television lacks. When a user selects a clip to watch, YouTube offers a sidebar listing similar videos that might also be of interest to the viewer. Visitors can leave comments after viewing a video or post their own video in response to one they've watched.

Another reason for YouTube's popularity is increased access to webcams that enable quick delivery of video content. Computer video cameras facilitate using the Quick Launch feature of YouTube that permits users to post videos to the site directly from the video camera, rather than creating a video and uploading it to YouTube. The capacity for immediacy and instantaneous feedback appeals to the sense of exigency that adolescents experience (Alverez, 1998).

Finally, YouTube has become more than a video sharing site, but also supplements social networking sites. For teens, video sharing on YouTube supports their social networks, as well as creating new connections and social networks (Lange, 2008). Creating and circulating videos can stimulate new relationships between those who make and those who circulate videos. Individuals who post thoughtful comments may prompt the video maker to respond to the poster. Commentators are often themselves video makers who post remarks with the strategic intent of forming relationships with others who will support their work (Lange, 2008).

INTERNET FAME

YouTube's slogan is "Broadcast Yourself," so it's no surprise that many teens submit user-generated video content to these sites. With the widespread popularity of camera phones, digital cameras, and other electronic devices, it's easy for amateurs to capture a moment of amusing pet antics or a skateboarding trick. Those with access to a webcam might record themselves telling a story, dancing, or singing along to a popular song.

Many young people create recordings for video sharing sites in the hope that their video might accrue enough views to become an online sensation, and that they might gain Internet celebrity. It may seem improbable, but the popularity of YouTube has given some degree of fame to some unlikely people. For example, Esmee Denters is a Dutch teen who posted YouTube videos of herself singing renditions of pop songs that were viewed by millions. As a result of her YouTube video, she received a record contract and a position as an opening act for the pop star Justin Timberlake.

VIRAL VIDEOS

Viral videos gain widespread popularity through Internet sharing. Many viral videos become widely known "memes," or often-repeated and circulated cultural items. Once a video reaches epidemic status, it might be featured on the home page of mainstream news sites, such as Yahoo.com, or receive attention from non-Internet media.

TV news programs have been known to devote segments to viral videos as fluff or filler. For example, the CNN news program *Anderson Cooper 360* regularly features a Dramatic Animal Video segment. This segment of the show was spurred by the popularity of the viral video "Dramatic Chipmunk," a short clip of a prairie dog on a Japanese TV show (www.youtube.com).

CAUTIONS FOR TEENS IN POSTING VIDEOS

Many viral videos are lighthearted and spread quickly because Internet users find them amusing enough to share. This phenomenon can have negative consequences, however, especially for teens. Unlike television productions, there are no checks to verify the consent of those who appear in web videos. Several of the most popular viral videos were dispersed without the consent of their stars and resulted in their humiliation.

Two videos in particular that were done by teens were appreciated for their unintended comedic value, and brought shame and derision rather than fame and fortune to their unwitting stars. One of these videos is Star Wars Kid (www.youtube.com), which was first posted on the Internet in 2002 and received an estimated 900 million views (BBC News, 2006). This video features an overweight 14-year-old boy who videotaped himself at his high school's video studio wielding a golf ball retriever as it if were a weapon from the *Star Wars* movies. The boy's video was found in the studio by his classmates and dispersed online through a peer-to-peer file-sharing application. Within 2 weeks, it was downloaded by several million people. The boy, derided by his peers, dropped out of school and needed psychiatric care. His parents filed a lawsuit against his classmates who uploaded the video because of the harassment and anguish the boy suffered as a result.

The popularity of another viral video known as Numa Numa Dance (www.youtube.com) foisted unwanted attention upon a 19-year-old in New Jersey who recorded himself lip-synching and dancing awkwardly to a Romanian pop song. He uploaded this video to the Internet, where it was viewed and ridiculed by millions of people when a popular website, www.ewsgrond.com, featured a link to it.

These examples demonstrate that teens must be cautious about the video content that they create, particularly those that they post online. These videos are reminders of the power of cyberbullies, a topic that should be discussed among teachers, parents, and teens. We advocate that adults remind teens to ask themselves if they would want their videos shared in later years with potential employers or other unintended audiences.

TEACHERTUBE

TeacherTube (www.teachertube.com) is a variation of YouTube that was launched in March 2007 as an online space for educators to share instructional videos and other videos related to education. Rather than posting their videos to YouTube, where they would surely be lost in the shuffle of millions of other videos, the creators constructed this space for teachers to support technology in the classroom and share information and lessons that cater to the digital learner. The site's creators cite statistics about Internet use and explain how popular technologies can not only increase students' interest in content concepts and heighten retention of information, but also effectively engage students in their own learning.

In 2007, TeacherTube partnered with the educational technology company Interwrite to hold a contest giving students the opportunity to create and submit music videos about how technology improves their learning in classrooms. The 2007 contest winner, a video titled, "Ain't Gonna Hold Us Back D-I-G-I-T-A-L (www.vopod.com) was created by students in a first-grade classroom in New York. A parody of the Gwen Stefani song "Hollaback Girl," the video not only demonstrates the importance of technology in the classroom, but also highlights the gender disparity in the technology world.

OTHER VIDEO SHARING SITES

Formerly known as GodTube, Tangle (www.tangle.com) offers faith-based and family-friendly social networking spaces for individuals, families, churches, and religious musical groups. The site extends video sharing to offer blog space and social networking applications. One of their popular videos is one called "Baby Got Book" by Dan Smith. This video parodies the popular rap song "Baby Got Back" by humorously changing the lyrics from the original (a lighthearted ode to attractive women) to a theme of admiration for girls who read the Bible (www.tangle.com).

VIDEO BLOGGING

Video blogging, sometimes referred to as vlogging, is video as a blogging medium. Like bloggers, vloggers record entries regularly, and often combine embedded video or a video link with text, still images, or metadata (comments about the file, such as key words). Vlogging has increased in popularity since 2005, with the proliferation of portable video recorders like the iPhone. Now there is a national conference for video bloggers called Vloggercon and awards for the best video blogs, the Vloggies.

Video blogging is an extension of the self-publishing phenomenon that also includes bloggers. Like blogging, adolescents use vlogging for personal expression and reflection. The ease and speed of authoring promotes a community that may critique one another's work. Because vlogging can be done without words, vlogging can promote global communication among teens. Vlogging may be used by students to record lectures or other class activities or can be used for digital storytelling (www.educause.edu/eli).

LITERACY SKILLS AND
ABILITIES IN VIDEO SHARING

There are numerous literacy skills and abilities associated with video consumption and production. Although it would appear that watching a video online is a passive activity, in fact, adolescents are actively interpreting and inferring messages from their content (Lange, 2008). Those who create their own videos are actively engaged in meaning-making processes that may require integrating texts and graphics with audio and visual texts.

There are also traditional literacy skills associated with video consumption and production. Participants in the video sharing community must acquire and understand a specific vocabulary (Xu, 2008). These terms include such concepts as embedding video; playlists (lists of audio and/or video files); and APIs (Application Program Interfaces), a set of tools for building program applications. These terms describe concepts that are shared among video users and producers who are members the video sharing community.

Suggestions for Teaching with Online Videos

- Science teachers could videotape lectures, demonstrations, or experiments and post them on TeacherTube. Students could refer to them at home in the event of absence or for help with homework. Providing taped lessons on TeacherTube also gives parents the opportunity to keep up with what their children are learning in school, help with homework, and expand on lessons at home.
- Art teachers might have students create a slideshow of their work, perhaps set to music, to place on YouTube. This would be an especially relevant lesson for older high school students needing to photograph and organize their portfolios for admission applications to colleges and submission to galleries.
- Foreign language teachers might show their classes prescreened YouTube videos with or without subtitles in the language being studied. Real-life situations, news stories, or versions of popular movies and TV shows dubbed in a foreign language may be appropriate choices, but care must be taken that the audio quality is high enough for language learners to understand. Teachers might create a vocabulary list or quiz based on the videos.
- Social studies teachers, particularly civics teachers, might encourage students to record speeches for class elections and upload them to a class account.
- Film and theater teachers might ask students to record, upload, and comment on their own and one another's acting.
- English/Language Arts teachers might allow students the option of creating a documentary-style video instead of or in addition to a research or opinion paper. Adapting a research paper to documentary video format could be an extra credit assignment.
- Teachers in any content area could use a short, compelling video to introduce a lesson or demonstrate a real-world concept.
- Teachers in any content area could help students become informed consumers and determine which videos contain reliable information, when it is appropriate to use YouTube, and how to consider privacy and prudent use of video sharing sites.

CHAPTER 6

Informational Wikis and Online Resources

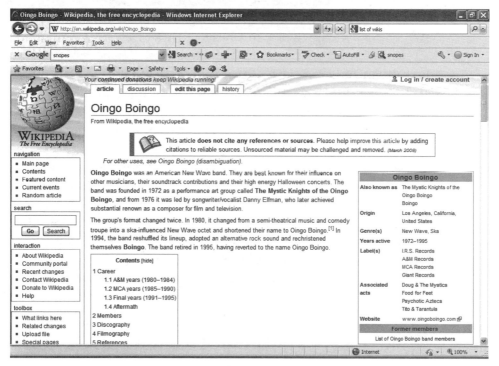

W ith so many media outlets available, including television, Internet publications, newspapers, and magazines, adolescents have vast amounts of information at their fingertips. Navigating and evaluating that information, conducting research, and crafting compelling and well-informed arguments are a central part of a student's education. Perhaps the most easily accessible source of information to help many adolescents with these skills is the Internet. Research indicates that what young people value most about the Internet is the ability it gives them to do research (Steward, 2007).

Traditionally, scientists, researchers, academics, and librarians have been entrusted to act as filters for the information that students consume. But with the Internet so accessible to many students, this tradition has changed drastically. The plethora of online collaborative resources makes it difficult for available knowledge to be vetted through official channels and has raised questions as to whether vetted information is really more reliable than information collected by volunteers.

WIKIS AS ONLINE SOURCES OF INFORMATION

A wiki (a Hawaiian word meaning "fast") is an easily learned, open-source software program that allows users to access and edit a text on an ongoing basis (Luce-Kapler & Dobson, 2005). These collaborative digital writing spaces allow multiple authors to edit and revise the same document simultaneously (Lewis, Leander, & Wang, 2007). Wikis both store and manage knowledge and are easily revised or removed.

Users can easily and quickly create new entries from a wiki launch pad. A user can create a page, click on the "edit this page" link, type in text or revisions, paste in images or links to other pages if desired, and save the work. Students can create wikis that provide information or develop hypertextual stories (Luce-Kapler, 2007) or other collaborative writing projects. In this chapter, we focus mainly on wikis as collaborative online sources of information.

WIKIPEDIA:
AUTHORING AND CO-AUTHORING KNOWLEDGE

Wikipedia's name is a *portmanteau* of two words, combining the terms *wiki* and *encyclopedia*. Wikipedia was created in 2001 as both an online community and an ever-expanding encyclopedia composed of free content crafted by volunteers. All content is stored, maintained, and available for use online and can be changed or updated by anyone.

Controversy Surrounding Wikipedia

Since its inception, Wikipedia has had its share of detractors. When it exploded in popularity, the accessibility and communal quality proved to be both an asset and a liability. Articles could be added and edited by anyone who visited the site. This free-for-all led to articles filled with bias, inaccurate information, and unverifiable sources. Wikipedia's founders have since established a system to help ensure the quality of articles, but critics remain unconvinced. Opponents frown on "crowdsourcing" (gathering collective knowledge from amateurs), believing that an encyclopedia compiled by the lay public cannot provide the same quality of information as one written by experts. Wikipedia does, however, enforce standards for the neutrality and verifiability of their sources. Although Wikipedia's content is monitored by moderators, anonymous editing is still possible. This means that despite their guidelines, concerns about Wikipedia's content are not unfounded. Unethical tampering with passages to make them less neutral is known to happen.

There is, however, an online application known as WikiScanner (www.wikiscanner.virgil.gr/) that tracks the IP addresses of anonymous editors and documents cases where unethical edits may have occurred. For example, an edit of a page pertaining to the Wal-Mart Corporation that resulted in more positive wording in a section on employee wages was shown to have originated from the company's own corporate headquarters (Borland, 2007).

In addition to articles on general subjects and historical topics, this online encyclopedia is quickly updated with information on developing trends. Because information can be added in the time it takes to write a paragraph, breaking news about most topics is generally incorporated into Wikipedia within hours, sometimes minutes, of the event. Popular culture figures, like characters from the television show *The Simpsons*, and trends that would not warrant inclusion in a print encyclopedia often receive lengthy and detailed articles in Wikipedia. Wikipedia also includes information on Internet fads, slang, and memes. While articles of this type would make print encyclopedias cluttered, unwieldy, and quickly out of date, they add to Wikipedia's value as a casual research tool.

Limitations to Using Reference Wikis

There is evidence to support that other electronic and print encyclopedias may also contain misinformation, misleading statements, or outright errors. In 2005, the journal *Nature* published an article asserting that Wikipedia was very close to *Encyclopedia Britannica* in accuracy, based on original research conducted by *Nature*'s staff

(Giles, 2005). *Encyclopedia Britannica* vehemently denied this and called for *Nature* to retract some of their statements. *Nature* issued a firm response confirming the accuracy of its research and refused to retract any part of the article. That two academic publishers can heatedly disagree about the accuracy of factual information means that all information, regardless of its source, should be carefully evaluated.

OTHER ONLINE RESOURCES

While the most popular, Wikipedia is far from the only free informational resource found online. Wikipedia's usefulness and popularity have spawned imitators and competitors that offer a different angle on the free online encyclopedia. For example, Conservapedia (www.conservapedia.com) is a wiki-style reference created because some political conservatives perceived that Wikipedia showed a liberal bias. While it is not nearly as carefully edited or comprehensive as Wikipedia, its articles about people and concepts have a slant that appeals to many Christian conservatives.

Other useful online resources include:

- **Goodreads** (www.goodreads.com) is a book-related reference site with social networking aspects. Members can search for information about books and authors, create and answer trivia questions, rate and review books, maintain lists of books that they plan to read and have read, and view and comment on the booklists and reviews of their friends and other site members.
- **Internet Movie Database** (www.imdb.com) is an exhaustive directory of information related to movies, actors, filmmakers, and anything associated with cinema.
- **LibraryThing** (www.librarything.com) is a combination of a reference and a social networking site in which site members create a searchable online catalog of books that they own or have read. They have the option to tag, review, and add pertinent information about their books, and view other members' libraries and discuss books.
- **Snopes** (www.snopes.com) is a helpful site to search to confirm or debunk an urban legend or rumor. Each page features a well-researched article about the origins of an urban legend, the verdict on its veracity or falsehood, and ideas about why so many people believe it.

SUPPORT FOR USING WIKIS IN CLASSROOMS

Teachers may have administrators who can or have established wikis for classroom use. If not, educators can create a class wiki free of charge through the site PBworks.com (www.pbworks.com), formerly known as PBwiki.com. This online space offers unlimited storage and document management for short-term use by educators.

LITERACY SKILLS AND ABILITIES FOSTERED BY WIKIS

Wikis help students develop and practice their skills as co-authors and collaborative writers. As content development and management technologies, wikis enable interactive and intercreative engagement (Duffy & Bruns, 2006). They help students develop thinking and writing skills that allow for inclusion and understanding of varying viewpoints, writing styles, and perspectives that may differ from their own through group consensus, inclusion, and compromise (Datman, 2005).

Students learn metacognitive thinking while writing, editing, and revising in a group context. Wikis facilitate writing in hybrid forms by incorporating links, graphics, and adding to or modifying the work of others in nonlinear and nonsequential forms. Writing with wikis can encourage connectivity and intertexuality by responding to and linking texts (Luce-Kapler, 2007).

Suggestions for Teaching with
Online Information Resources in Content Areas

It is generally agreed upon by the academic community that Wikipedia should not be cited as a source for students' papers. Wikipedia's founder, Jimmy Wales, has warned students not to cite Wikipedia when doing academic research (Young, 2006). Wikipedia has a page dedicated to its own academic use (www.en.wikipedia.org/wiki/Wikipedia:Academic_use). This page stresses that any encyclopedia, whether print- or web-based, is a starting point rather than an ending point for research, and that it is necessary to verify information by checking an authoritative source.

Wikis are so common as to be nearly inescapable. Students will need to be taught how to use them responsibly, and will need to know that they need to verify the quality of their information no matter where they find it. Wikis can be a valuable resource when used with a critical eye. As the debate over whether information from Wikipedia should be accepted as research for assignments continues, there are other ways to use the concepts behind Wikipedia, as well as the tool itself.

- Mathematics teachers could have their students each write an article explaining a specific concept and post their articles to a class wiki that could serve as a troubleshooting guide.
- As information management becomes an even more important part of operating an effective company, business teachers could teach students how to use technology like wikis to store information, emphasizing the digital skills and the planning and communication skills that are needed for online information storage and retrieval.
- Science students could collaborate on a wiki by having one student write a post explaining a scientific concept, such as Boyle's law. Other students could add to the wiki by adding related laws or underlying concepts, such as Charles's law.
- Social studies or science teachers could have their classes keep a wiki as a collaborative, online study group. Students could record concepts from each day's lesson, with each class member adding information to the wiki and then reviewing the wiki at the end of a unit in preperation for the unit test.
- English/Language Arts teachers could discuss the debate over accuracy of information as a useful lead-in to teaching critical thinking skills. Teachers could instruct students in ways to examine media with a critical lens by verifying information and detecting bias. Critical analyses might not be limited to controversial sources such as Wikipedia, but could include other media, including books, advertisements, television commercials, and newspaper reports.
- English/Language Arts teachers could model how to critically read a Wikipedia article and interrogate the text.
- English/Language Arts teachers could show students how to do bibliographical branching by exploring an article's bibliography for sources that can provide more in-depth information and teach students how to crtically evaluate those sources.

- Social studies teachers might have students use Wikipedia as a quick way to find common facts or gain information when a text makes a reference to an unfamiliar person or event. For example, a student who forgets the year when the Spanish-American War took place might use Wikipedia to refresh his or her memory.
- English/Language Arts teachers might teach students how to use online resources for quick definitions of terms or to search for details about authors. For example, those who are unfamiliar with the writer Ring Lardner might glance at the Wikipedia page about him to make sense of frequent references to him in *The Catcher in the Rye* by J. D. Salinger, a novel commonly assigned to students in high school English classes.

CHAPTER 7

Fan Fiction, Fan Art, and Web Comics

Fandom, the act of being a fan, is a large part of youth culture. Fandom is also known as participatory culture (Jenkins, 2006). One way that young people formulate their identities is by associating themselves with the music, books, television, and movies that are most relevant to their lives. A person's interests can help to define his or her identity. Whether it's a kindergartner's *Dora the Explorer* sneakers or an anime figure doodled on a high schooler's binder cover, fandom gives kids a way to find common ground with others.

FAN FICTION

Fan fiction is creative writing based on the characters or settings of books, television shows, movies, comics, and video games. Because there are so many types of media that garner fan fiction, from this point on we refer to the various subjects of fandom as a "series." While fan fiction was once distributed mainly through photocopied zines or self-publications (see Chapter 8), it is now propagated almost exclusively online. Because of copyright issues, fan art and fan fiction must be distributed without profit. There are websites devoted to fan fiction of any series. FanFiction.net (www.fanfiction.net) is the largest of these. There are also countless fan-managed sites and groups on blog sites such as LiveJournal that are dedicated to the fandom of just one series.

Certain series undoubtedly lend themselves to fan-made material more than others. Science fiction, fantasy, manga (Japanese comics in a particular style), and anime (Japanese animation) receive an overwhelming share of attention because the characters and plots capture the imaginations of young people. The most popular fan fictions are writings that extend animes, like *Sailor Moon* and *Naruto*; books, like the *Harry Potter* and *Twilight* series; TV shows, such as *CSI*, *Doctor Who*, and *Buffy the Vampire Slayer*; and role-playing video games, including *Final Fantasy* and *Zelda*. These series garner lots of fan activity because they have characters that fans can relate to emotionally and a focus on relationships between characters that are compelling yet indistinct enough to make speculation fun. Each one of these has thousands, if not tens of thousands, of stories listed on FanFiction.net and thousands more that are archived on sites devoted to specific series.

Many fan-created stories center on romantic and/or sexual relationships that are not part of the series' canon. The majority of these imagined relationships are between two male characters. This is known as "slash fiction." Stories that feature relationships between two women are called "femslash" and are less common. These stories are often sexually explicit so care must be taken before encouraging students to seek out fan fiction as part of an assignment.

The phenomenon of teenagers creating fan fiction on their own is very common. Fiction shared online ranges from amateurish first attempts riddled with spelling and punctuation errors to professional-quality work. Fan fiction accomplishes the formidable task of getting otherwise academically unmotivated teenagers to read and write outside school. The majority of authors and readers of fan fiction are female, most of them in their late teens and early twenties. Teens may be hesitant to discuss their fan fiction with adults or their friends, either because they are shy about sharing it or because they fear that their fandom might be considered silly, nerdy, or frivolous.

In the anonymous world of the Internet, teens delight in reading, sharing, editing, commenting on, and receiving feedback on their fan fiction. Most sites allow members who are willing to proofread and suggest improvements for the stories of other fans to be listed as beta-readers on the site or in their profile. If the author desires, he or she may contact a beta-reader and ask for edits on his or her story. The beta-reader might proofread the first draft of a story or provide feedback throughout the process of writing a multi-chapter story. Authors and their beta-readers usually discuss their work through e-mail or instant messaging, and it is customary for authors to thank their beta-reader publicly on the site when they post their stories.

Stories may be single-chapter "oneshots," multi-chapter series, or even novel-length sagas. Generally with longer stories, the author will post chapters as they are finished in the manner of a serialized story in a magazine. When posting a story to a fan site, the author designates a genre (e.g., humor, drama, romance) and includes content warnings (e.g., violence, swearing, sex, character death). When a story or chapter is posted, the author receives instant feedback from other fans in the form of comments or reviews of their story.

Fan fiction is just one way that young people explore fandom. Some people, known as "character bloggers," maintain an online journal or profile on a social networking site that "belongs to" the character of their choice. This is a way for fans to role play the character and to interact in character with other role players in the fandom.

FAN ART

Another important aspect of fandom is fan art, visual art depicting characters or scenes related to a series. Like fan fiction, there are sites devoted mainly to displaying fan art. The most popular of these are Deviantart (www.deviantart.com) and Fan Art Central (www.fanart-central.net). Other sites and forums devoted to a particular series will typically have a section devoted to fan art.

The quality of the art found on these sites runs the gamut from pencil doodles on notebook paper to beautiful and impressively rendered works. A wide variety of forms and media are represented, such as drawings, paintings, sculpture, photography, digital art, and comics.

In addition, "cosplay," short for "costume role-play," may be considered a type of fan art. Particularly popular in anime, science fiction, and manga fandom, cosplay is a type of performance art in which fans create and dress in costumes resembling their favorite characters. Sometimes these fans enact scenes from a series with other cosplayers. This activity is common at anime, gaming, and comic book conventions. Many fans take special care to resemble their character as much as possible, with some very elaborate and impressive costumes.

WEB COMICS

Comics can be another type of fandom. There several genres of comics, including superhero comics; science fiction; realistic fiction; fantasy; humor; action/adventure; horror/supernatural; life stories; and manga, or comics that conform to a Japanese style developed in the late 20th century. Almost any teenager who loves comics will try to draw his or her own at some point. With the wide availability of computers and the Internet, creating and distributing comics has never been easier.

In the past, most people consumed comics by purchasing single comic books at a store or by reading them in the daily paper. But as hard copy newspapers' circulation decreases, comic fans are not satisfied with the comic strips of the daily paper, and the major comic book companies maximize profits by producing only a few genres of comics. Young people who love comics but aren't excited about what's available via mainstream outlets are increasingly turning to the Internet. The future, and perhaps the present, of comics is online.

Creating and distributing comics online has several advantages. Web comics let artists be creative in determining the size, form, and content of their comics. Web comics are able to exist far beyond the limitations of traditional print comics. Unlike syndicated cartoonists, when an artist publishes a comic on his or her website, the work becomes accessible to the largest possible audience. Comics that are too bizarre to be marketable can exist and garner fans online. Artists can work without an editor or a deadline, make comics as large as they wish, and publish in full color at no additional cost. They also receive the benefit of instant feedback on their work. Artists can enable viewers to leave comments on each comic or set up a web forum on their website for fans to discuss their comics.

Young people who love comics will always create them for their own amusement. Many budding comic artists draw them the old-fashioned way, with a pencil and paper. These print comics can be scanned and then touched up and/or colored with photo editing software for easy online sharing. It may be simpler for tech-savvy amateur artists to draw comics digitally in programs like Microsoft Paint or Photoshop. It's easy to make quick sketches and erase mistakes in the digital medium.

Sequential art is a broad medium and drawing skills are not necessary to create a successful comic. Some humorous comics can be made by using images acquired from Google searches. Photographically inclined artists can snap photographs of their friends acting out a scene and add text bubbles with photo editing software.

FIGURE 7.1. A comic created in Microsoft Paint by a high school freshman, Nora. She created this cartoon to spoof the Little Mermaid story, which implies that girls should be feminine, princesslike, and aspire to marry a prince.

Popular Web Comics

Some popular comics crafted with minimal drawing include Dinosaur Comics (www.qwantz.com/), which features pixilated dinosaurs having amusing discussions, and uses the same six-panel image for every strip; xkcd (www.xkcd.com/), a humorous, geeky math-, science-, and technology-themed comic that uses only crude stick figures; and PartiallyClips (www.partiallyclips.com), which uses only clip art from a royalty-free collection and has no recurring characters. Readers can keep track of which online comics have been updated by using the WebComic List (www.webcomiclist. com), which keeps track of 14,000 web comics several times a day.

Support for Making Web Comics

Anyone can create a comic by using a cartoon strip generator such as Tondoo (www.tondoo.com), Stripgenerator (www.strip generator.com), or MakeBeliefsComix (www.makebeliefscomix. com). These sites enable artists to arrange pre-made backgrounds, characters, and objects, and to type their own text in word bubbles. Some of the most popular web comic artists craft their images without drawing by reusing clip-art–like images interspersed with original text.

Scratch Projects

Scratch is a new programming language that makes it easy for teens to create comics, interactive stories, animations, video games, music, art, and birthday cards and share them on the web (www. scratch.mit.edu). Scratch was developed by researchers at the Massachusetts Institute of Technology's media lab and is funded by the National Science Foundation. Scratch is available free of charge and can be accessed globally in various languages.

LITERACY SKILLS AND ABILITIES FOSTERED BY FAN FICTION, FAN ART, AND COMICS

Adolescents who compose fan fiction may also engage in complementary role-playing; each genre of narrative can reinforce the composition skills of the other. Writing and role-playing fan fiction

Figure 7.2. Bwobs is a Scratch video game Quinn created about a beige Bwob on a quest to save the world by destroying evil red Bwobs who want to enslave Bwob-manity.

can aide in fostering and practicing students' writing skills and abilities. These include developing characters through use of adverbs and adjectives, changing voice and dialogue from narrator to character, crafting intricate plots, editing, and writing in the fantasy genre (Thomas, 2007).

In addition to fostering students' learning and practicing of these skills, fan fiction may support the acquisition of other literacy skills. ELL learners writing fan fiction and song fiction (stories based on the lyrics of a song) learn to access multiple texts and write in hybrid forms by integrating popular culture resources in linguistic and audio modes (Black, 2008).

Adolescents use fan fiction to project their identities and social affiliations (Black, 2008). Fan fiction readers and writers understand and make use of intertextuality. They understand the relationships and references between and among texts of the fan writers' stories and the original media texts. They create complex texts by blending elements from various genres, such as fantasy, science fiction, and romance (Chandler-Olcott & Mahar, 2003).

Creating fan art, comics, and animations through web-based programs like Scratch can help young people to develop 21st-century learning skills. By creating and sharing with Scratch, students learn to communicate clearly, use technologies fluently, and design iteratively. Creating and sharing Scratch projects can foster students' learning of mathematical and computational ideas while also learning to think creatively, reason systematically, and work collaboratively.

Creating comics can help young people tap into their creativity and practice their language and storytelling abilities. Authoring comics may help young people to find their voice and express themselves through writing. Brainstorming, outlining, sketching, and writing original comic books have helped adolescents to author their lives as urban youth (Bitz, 2004).

Comics have been powerful means and motivators for students in learning literacy skills and abilities. Students authoring, reading, and discussing comics learn and practice skills of debate, discussion, and critique (Norton, 2003). Authoring comics can help teachers address the state standards for reading, writing, listening, and speaking and develop their abilities with literary response, expression, critical analysis and evaluation, and social interaction (Bitz, 2004). Producing comics has taught students vocabulary related to the genre of comics, such as panels and inking, and terms related to art, such as perspective and design (Bitz, 2004). Reading and creating comics like manga can help students to acquire content vocabulary and knowledge about other countries (Botzakis, 2008). Proficient manga readers develop their skills with and are adept at interpreting graphical information as well as printed texts (Schwartz & Rubinstein-Avilla, 2006).

Suggestions for Teaching with Fan Fiction, Fan Art, and Web Comics in Content Areas

Maintaining familiarity with youth culture is an effective way for teachers to build positive relationships with their students. Teachers can let their students know if they are familiar with the bands their students like, saw the same movie over the weekend as they did, or have read the latest popular young adult novel. Aside from these general suggestions, we offer the following ideas for capitalizing on students' fandom and artistic inclinations in content teaching:

- Art teachers could have students create a three-dimensional sculpture depicting their favorite two-dimensional comic character.
- English/Language Arts teachers could ask students to create a superhero-style comic centered on a myth or a legend that shows their comprehension of the story's moral.
- Social studies teachers teaching civics might assign students to compose a political cartoon about a current issue. For bonus points, students could be encouraged to submit them to the school newspaper.
- English/Language Arts teachers might make copies of a few pages from comic books with the text removed and ask students to compose and share their own story lines for creative writing.
- English/Language Arts teachers could have students write fan fiction for a book, movie, or game that they like. Students could write a chapter that picks up where the story left off, compose an alternate ending, or write their interpretation of an event from the book.

CHAPTER 8

Zines and Indie Music

W hen young people cannot find commercial magazines, books, or music that speak to them, they often create their own. Adolescents have strong needs to see themselves reflected in the media that they consume and seek lyrical, print, and electronic texts that they can relate to as they are developing their identities. When traditional media sources fail to address young people's interests and desires, many youth enact the ethos of do-it-yourself by creating their own alternative texts.

ZINES

One unique type of DIY media is zines (pronounced "zeens"). Zines are self-published booklets containing material generated by amateur writers and artists who are referred to as "zinesters." Zines are commonly, but not exclusively, produced by adolescents and young adults in their twenties. A zine may be written, assembled, duplicated, and distributed by one person or the joint effort of a group of friends or like-minded acquaintances.

In the past 30 years, zines have become most closely associated with music fandom, but they have their roots in science fiction fandom. The word "zine" is derived from "fanzine," which in turn is short for "fan magazine." Fanzines became popular in the 1930s, and were typically based on superhero comic books and typed and reproduced on lithograph machines (Row, 1997).

Today's zines may be personal (e.g., poetry and prose), political (e.g., feminist or anarchist), or hobby zines (e.g., crafting, skateboarding, or fishing). Zines may appear in hard-copy form, or they may be e-zines available only online.

Zines are distributed mostly within communities that support their focus. For example, music-related zines are distributed in hard copy at record stores and concerts. Politically oriented zines are often available at infoshops, places that combine a radical bookstore with a movement archive (www.infoshop.org). Science fiction, art, and comic zines are frequently left at underground bookstores and comic book stores.

Zines of all types can be obtained by mail order on the Internet through distros, or online distribution centers. Some zinesters maintain their own websites that may offer additional content to complement their zine, information on ordering a paper copy of their zine, or an online zine. There are websites that maintain lists of contact information so that site visitors can e-mail or write the creator to request a copy of the zine through the mail. Depending on the cost of production and the zinester's financial situation, zines are usually free or cost a small fee, such as $1, some stamps, or another zine.

Zines are most commonly pieced together from cut-out texts (handwritten, typed, or printed from a computer) and images pasted on backgrounds (such as pictures from magazines). The originals are photocopied, which creates a distinctive high-contrast, black-and-white aesthetic. More inventive zinesters take advantage of this by incorporating interesting textures, sewing through the paper, or attaching small objects to the pages.

Why Do Adolescents Write Zines?

Uncensored, intensely personal self-expression is inherent in zining. Creating a zine can be a highly rewarding activity for those motivated to express themselves and forge an individual identity related to his or her interests.

Zinesters often craft their zines as a rebellion against and in place of commercial texts. They take up topics not often found in the commercial press or teen magazines. They may write against social injustices, such as homophobia, racism, sexism, and classism, that they experience firsthand or vicariously through others' experiences or through the media. They may write about political issues, feminist issues, or personal issues, such as date rape, self-injurious behavior, or anorexia. Their writings may stimulate online or off-line discussions with others on these topics and help zinesters to form new social networks.

Zines can also serve as celebrations of popular culture and focus on music, humor, and entertainment. Zinesters often compose personal zines that are compilations of their own poetry and prose. Other zines are edited collections that include multiple authors' writings as well.

Zines in themselves are a form of community with a large network of producers and consumers. Zining can offer an outlet, encouragement, and other social supports in place of or in addition to those provided by family, friends, and classmates. This community can be very important for youth who may feel otherwise isolated. Even those with strong emotional support and a healthy social circle may find the draw of a vast zine community very enticing. The zine community gives young people access to perspectives and friendships across the world.

Limitations to Using Zines in the Classroom

As members of the community of those who read and/or write zines, we caution that zines are not appropriate as in-school reading or writing assignments. Zines, by nature, commonly contain strong language, frank opinions, themes, illustrations, and photographs that are not "school-appropriate." For these reasons, zines do not belong in classrooms.

In addition, zinesters themselves protest the co-opting or insti-
tutionalizing of zines in school (Guzzetti & Gamboa, 2005c). Zines
are created for the fun of writing with no restrictions; for the ability
to break the rules of academic writing, such as the five-paragraph
essay; and for the freedom they allow of self-expression and artistic
creation through mixing graphics and texts. Assigning students to
make a zine to be judged and graded will likely result in students
having to censor themselves, thereby rendering zines just another
ordinary assignment. Like Knobel and Lankshear (2001), we fear
that making zines writing assignments would result in texts that
were produced according to someone else's vision and purpose
rather the zinester's own. Rather, we offer suggestions below for
incorporating the ethos and elements of zines as ways to motivate
and foster students' writing for self-expression.

INDIE MUSIC

The DIY movement has its roots in indie, or independent, music.
There are several genres of indie music that speak to adolescents'
needs for alternative music that is not commercially produced.
Here, we discuss three kinds of indie music: punk rock, hip-hop,
and video game music. Through creating these genres of music,
students are enabled "to draw from their own cultural understandings of language, participation, and power" (Majors, Kim, & Ansari, 2009, p. 353) to produce lyrical texts.

Punk Rock

Punk rock is characterized by loud, fast-paced rhythms and
anti-authoritarian lyrical content, reflecting the subculture's wish to
escape society's notions of acceptable behavior (Row, 1997). Punk
rock is known for its freedom of expression, encouraging young
people to create their own musical texts as empowerment of the
individual and expression of personal identity.
        There are several genres of punk rock, including political punk,
emo or emotional punk, and feminist punk or "riot grrrl." Many
punk songs are harsh political or emotional outcries of rebellion
(Desmond, 1987). Punk is valued more for its creative and empow-
ering processes and effects than for its technical prowess. Punk as

a genre of music and an act of transformation is considered a form of free speech representing how individuals want to live and take action in the world.

The music that adolescents enjoy, like punk rock, is often complex, richly metaphoric, and symbolic. Young people make their own connections between the lyrical texts they enjoy outside of school and their academic instruction (Guzzetti & Yang, 2005), supporting the idea that music is a logical bridge between popular culture and academic instruction (Duncan-Andrade & Morrell, 2000).

Hip-Hop and Freestyling

Hip-hop culture is fashionable with a diverse group of adolescents and is very popular because it can be created with a minimum of equipment. The term "hip-hop," which is frequently used interchangeably with "rap," refers to music with lyrics that are recited rather than sung either over an instrumental beat or unaccompanied. Hip-hop culture has impacted the lives of working-class youth (Morrell & Duncan-Andrade, 2008). Hip-hop fandom leads many young people to engage in the DIY practice known as freestyling. Freestyling is improvisation by reciting rhymes either unaccompanied or over music from a turntable, computer, CD player, MP3 player, or even a friend's beatbox rhythm. Becoming skilled at freestyling requires much practice, and it can be a status symbol to produce the most impressive rhymes. While some youth make audio or video recordings of themselves freestyling, it is not a necessary part of the art form. In fact, the ephemeral nature of spontaneously created lyrics is part of the appeal.

Video Game Music

Because music is a prominent aspect of video games, fandom of video game music is as natural as fandom of the games themselves. Any video game fan who picks up a musical instrument may be tempted to bang out a tune from his or her favorite game, and some of those who do end up making a hobby or a career out of it. While video game music fandom is still a fringe pursuit, it is becoming more recognized with the increasing popularity of gaming and the rising nostalgia for older console games.

There are several approaches that video game fans take to express their fandom through creating music. One approach is to form a band that plays renditions of video game songs on rock instruments such as guitars, drums, and keyboards. One of the best examples of these bands is the Phoenix-based band the Minibosses (www.minibosses.com). Members of The Minibosses arrange and play game songs and medleys note for note on their instruments. As game music is generally instrumental, there often is no vocalist. Other bands create lyrics to go along with the game music that they play and/or experiment with and expand upon the melodies from the video game songs to create game-inspired songs like the Los Angeles band the Megas (www.themegas.com), who play only covers (music first performed and popularized by other artists) of the CAPCOM-published NES game *Mega Man 2*. Video game bands like these have followings, and they frequently perform at video game, comic book, and other popular culture conventions.

Chiptunes

Chiptunes are songs made by using the sound chips from video game consoles and computers instead of using traditional musical instruments and synthesizers. Chiptunes can be created and played on video game hardware with the help of software that allows users to sequence the sounds contained on the game system's chip.

Chiptune artists also use computer programs that allow them to create music on an emulated version of the system's sound chip, and then export code that is playable as a song on the game system itself. Most of this software was developed by game music fans and is available for free on the Internet. Anyone with access to a computer and a real fondness for video game music can create a chiptune.

Circuit Bending

Video game music fans can physically modify game systems to turn them into musical instruments. This practice, called circuit bending, is not limited to video game systems, but can be done with almost any electronic item that makes a sound. An example is shown in Figure 8.1, which pictures a modified Atari 2600 game system. When buttons on the control pads are pressed, they pro-

FIGURE 8.1. A modded Atari 2600 game system created by noted circuit bender Corey Busboom.

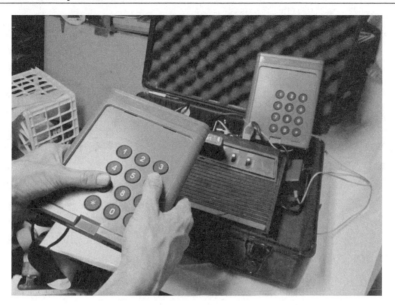

duce electronic tones. Pressing the system's buttons in a sequence can produce a melody reminiscent of the songs from actual Atari games. While circuit bending is a rather obscure art form, it can be a very stimulating way for an electronics-savvy instructor to give students a hands-on understanding of electronic circuits in physics class.

LITERACY SKILLS AND ABILITIES FOSTERED BY ZINES AND INDIE MUSIC

Young people authoring zines display a wide variety of textual forms and writing styles. In creating backgrounds and borders for their writings, they select from and use a diverse array of texts and images. These include advertisements, product labels, magazine pages, Internet graphics, newspaper excerpts, photographs, and hand-drawn illustrations. Their pages are characterized by collage and pastiche as they form their writings from print texts, images, and hyperlinks that are carefully and strategically placed together in complementary artistic and semiotic ways.

Zinesters write in a variety of genres, including poems, narratives, essays, journal entries, and instructional texts (Knobel & Lankshear, 2001), for a variety of purposes. Zinesters have been characterized as being "tactically" competent writers whose zines are "vibrant, volatile, thriving social practices that describe deep currents and concerns within youth culture" (Knobel & Lankshear, 2001, p. 172). In this cursory review of the literacy skills and strategies that young people employ in zining, we do not intend to underestimate the underlying strategic thinking and tactical competencies inherent in zining. These abilities may also include writing with creative subversion, scamming resources like copy machine access, appropriating writing styles and texts, deconstructing texts, and reassembling materials to produce new media (Kearney, 2006a; Knobel & Lankshear, 2001).

Creating indie music requires a variety of literacy skills and abilities. Young people transpose written texts to oral texts, develop storytelling skills, and produce collaborative writings. They write in a variety of genres, fostering metacognitive thinking about and critical reflection on their written products. They take critical perspectives and write creatively in ways that promote nonlinear thinking.

Suggestions for Teaching with Indie Music and Zines in Content Areas

One of the best examples of a teacher appropriately incorporating indie media into his curriculum comes from an English/Language Arts teacher, Lance Balla, in Washington. Lance was teaching a unit on satire as a literary genre to his 12th-grade Advanced Placement class. One of the students' reading assignments was the satirical essay "A Modest Proposal" by Jonathan Swift. Written in 1729, Swift's essay mocked the abuses inflicted on Irish Catholics by well-to-do English Protestants who charged Irish farming families so much rent that they lived on the brink of starvation.

To relate this text to modern-day satire, Lance played the punk song "Kill the Poor" by the Dead Kennedys. He asked his students questions that helped them to interrogate the texts, discussing the lyrics and the ties between the two pieces, including their parallel satirical messages about the eradication of the poor, and the common delivery of those messages through parody and satire. Making connections between the two texts, one historical and one of current popular culture, helped the students to relate to the common ideas of social and political injustices and understand the literacy devices of parody, irony, wit, and satire that conveyed those ideas.

Below are other suggestions for incorporating the ethos of zines and indie music into classroom instruction:

- English/Language Arts teachers could encourage students to submit their artwork, poetry, essays, and short fiction and distribute these writings to the class.
- English/Language Arts teachers might invite those who create zines to speak to their classes about their zining practices to raise students' awareness of these alternative texts and related DIY media. Students could be engaged in a discussion in which individuals share their opinions about the underlying philosophy and spirit of DIY media.
- Music teachers might encourage students to compose their own music by downloading Mario Paint Composer (available free from www.unfungames.com/mariopaint/). This program provides an intuitive, fun way to compose music by arranging symbols, such as hearts, mushrooms, and airplanes, on a musical staff.
- Computer lab teachers and music teachers might download some samples and a sequencing program such as ModPlug Tracker (www.sourceforge.net/projects/modplug/) and encourage students to create chiptunes.
- English/Language Arts teachers might incorporate the ethos of zining by engaging students in critical writing workshops in which students read and discuss literature with social and political themes and use fiction writing to construct and analyze social justice issues (Cherland, 2009).

CHAPTER 9

DIY Media, Assessment, Achievement, and Ethics

No discussion of using adolescents' DIY media in the classroom and the literacy skills and strategies fostered by those practices would be complete without mention of how those literacy abilities are, are not, or may be assessed in schools. Others have noticed the gap between the explosion of new literacy practices and current assessment practices that reflect narrow definitions of literacy and constrain literacy instruction (e.g., Marshall, 2009; Santa, 2006). Assessment policies, approaches, and measures often have not kept up with the changing nature of literacy and what counts as literate practice in the 21st century.

STANDARDIZED ASSESSMENTS AND DIY MEDIA

New DIY media have extended the range and sophistication of students' literacy practices (Kist, 2005). Yet many school districts' assessment policies and measures constrain the curriculum and restrict the resources that teachers can use in working with adolescents (Marshall, 2009). It seems that testing practices discourage rather than encourage teachers' incorporation of DIY practices in classrooms.

Not only do traditional assessments that focus on print-based reading and writing constrain teachers in what literacy skills and abilities are fostered and how, they also are unfair to students. Those who do not perform well in academic settings with traditional forms of literate expression may be facile in their use of literacy practices for their own purposes in out-of-school settings (Knobel, 2001). In addition, low-achieving students may demonstrate complex understandings of the new literate skills and abilities inherent in new media practices that are not measured by traditional forms of assessment. High-stakes tests do not tap into the multiple and new literacies of adolescents as text producers, but rather position them as mere reproducers of texts (Anagnostopoulos, 2003).

As a result, many of the DIY media skills and abilities that we identified in past chapters remain unrecognized by standard assessments. These include text design and redesign skills inherent in such DIY practices as creating video games. Literate abilities underlying these processes include remixing (playing with text genres like manga and anime); using visuals for words; understanding the grammar of visual design; and using color, font, and flash media to design and redesign texts (Burke & Rowsell, 2007). These skills are embedded within a broader understanding of the underlying structures, discourses, and ideologies of these texts, but are typically not measured by standard assessments.

There is, however, some movement toward making national, state, and local assessments more authentic and representative of new literate practices. For example, the National Council of Teachers of English advocates multiple types of assessment in an assessing-to-learn model to reveal students' individual abilities (Hammett, 2007). The North Central Regional Laboratory reports that content standards are being redesigned in mathematics, science, geography, and art history, and as those standards are revised, new assessments will also be developed (www.ncrel.org). These new assessments will be based on the theory that what is assessed should be what is taught.

INFORMAL ASSESSMENTS
AS ALTERNATIVE ASSESSMENTS

One way that classroom teachers can tap into their students' literate abilities with DIY media is through informal assessments that acknowledge their students' complex literacy practices. Conley (2008) advises teachers to begin by determining what students know, what they know how to do, and what they care about doing. Informal assessments of students' interests and capabilities can enable teachers to determine the range of literate practices that individuals engage with in informal settings and help teachers to plan instruction that acknowledges young people's expertise with new media.

Questionnaires, Checklists, Interviews, and Writings

To this end, teachers can design their own assessments. These can be survey questionnaires or checklists that list the literacy practices presented in this text that would help teachers note students' applications of these skills and abilities. They can also be brief interview guides that allow students to identify their literate practices and describe what they actually do during those practices. These questions might be designed as follow-ups to students' responses to the questionnaires or checklists to provide more detail about the literate processes that students use to consume and produce DIY media and digital texts.

Teachers might also create writing assignments that give them insights into students' DIY media consumption and production. These might include asking students to write their literacy autobiographies or keep journals that document their out-of-school literacy practices (Conley, 2008). Journaling has been a successful strategy for discovering the hidden literacies in adolescents' lives (Bean, Bean, & Bean, 1998).

Criterion Reference Measures

Other efforts in changing assessments to reflect 21st-century literacies are more advanced outside the United States. Hammett (2007) reports success in Canada with developing criterion-referenced measures, or rubrics, for measuring students' abilities to read a range of texts. These measures assess students' abilities with multimodal and collaborative texts, and reflect a view of reading as an active process of constructing meaning from a wide range of text forms, including print, film, television, and electronic.

In these assessments, students read poems and narrative and informational texts with prose and illustrations, respond to visual advertisements, and demonstrate listening skills. Students respond to questions by writing, completing a chart, or drawing a picture or graphic. Items tap adolescents' abilities with informational texts, media, and visual texts. Test items assess students' abilities with critical literacies or thinking that involve questioning assumptions; investigating how language is constructed by social, historical, and economic contexts; and examining power relations in language. The texts for these assessments are multimodal and use a wide variety of features (e.g., words, color, images, fonts, and spacing) to convey messages and solicit students' knowledge. In this way, these tests assess students' abilities with multiliteracies and can be adapted for testing students' new literacies. Panels of teachers score these items by using rubrics developed for assessing students' abilities with reading, viewing, representing, and listening.

The interactive website www.learnrubric.ca offers support for teachers in Canada and other countries who are using rubrics or scoring guides to evaluate students' performance and assess reading, writing, visual literacy, and other skills. Links are provided to guidelines for constructing assessment rubrics, explanations of rubric construction, advantages of rubrics, and sample rubrics and templates. Links are also included to podcasts by experts in assessment who discuss related issues.

ETHICAL ISSUES IN TEACHING WITH DIY MEDIA

The process of making and sharing DIY media also creates ethical issues. The Web has made it easier for young people to become media authors and, in doing so, repurpose extant media. As a result, violation of copyright laws can be "just one mouse click away" (Peppler & Kafai, 2007b, p. 6).

User-created content brings up issues of authorship. Instead of being seen as sole intellectual property, DIY media are often thought of as commonly created. This view of authorship may apply to students who are modding video games; remixing media to create a YouTube video; or cutting and pasting newspaper articles, magazine ads, or labels to create a zine. These activities have implicit and unresolved issues of media ownership and control.

Creating DIY media can provide an appropriate balance in a culture of media consumption, so it is important that these issues be resolved and that all have access to participate in creating media. Although the boundaries between media consumer and producer are blurring, there is still a large chasm between those who own and control media and those who have the possibilities of creating them (Peppler & Kafai, 2007b).

An appropriate goal of literacy education for the new millennium should be to prepare students to become members of today's participatory culture. This goal implies educating students to critically examine and evaluate DIY media and consider issues of authorship, privacy, intent, self-representation, and content when producing their own media and sharing or modifying others' products. Students will need to understand these ethical issues when consuming or producing DIY new media for their own purposes.

How Teachers Can Address Ethical Issues of DIY Media

Teachers can address issues of access, authorship, identity, and critical consumption and production by helping students form ethical understandings. Teachers can provide students with the access necessary to consume and create new media by incorporating these new literacies into their instruction and assignments. Teachers can also allow individuals to share their DIY media products with one another to facilitate students' awareness of and access to these new media texts and practices.

Teachers can also engage students in critical reflection about these media texts and their participation in them. Students can be taught to ask themselves questions like, "Does copying or modifying this digital media infringe on anyone's rights?" "Am I violating anyone's privacy by posting or copying this?" "How do I represent myself in online spaces like my websites, my LiveJournal, or my page on MySpace?" Teachers can lead discussions with their students that address these questions as they interact with various DIY media texts. In doing so, teachers can guide their students to become reflective participants who understand the connections between the media skills they learn and their responsibilities as ethical consumers and producers of new media.

DIY MEDIA AND STUDENTS' ACHIEVEMENTS

In an atmosphere of high-stakes testing, teachers may wonder how incorporating DIY media, particularly digital DIY media, might help to improve students' achievement in reading and writing or subject matter, particularly as measured by test scores. Since using DIY media texts in classrooms is a relatively new practice, researchers are just beginning to address this question. Most researchers who have observed students using these media texts in classrooms have described how these practices engage and motivate students in their learning and instruction, but have not yet explored their impact on students' literacy or subject matter achievement (e.g., Kist, 2003; Luce-Kapler, 2007; Xu, 2008).

There is some evidence, however, that using and producing these new media not only engage and motivate students, but also lead to improving their literacy achievement. For example, middle school students who wrote and discussed their responses to literature online through digital software made gains in critical thinking skills and improved their perceptions of themselves as writers (Wolsey & Grisham, 2007). Fourth-grade students who completed problem-based writing and descriptive writing activities in a virtual world significantly improved their achievement on standardized writing measures (Warren, Dondlinger, & Barab, 2008). These students chose to spend far more time practicing their writing than students who were not able to use the virtual environment. Increased time practicing their writing may also have led to increases in students' writing achievement.

Other researchers have documented how consuming and producing DIY media results in improved achievement in subject matter concepts. For example, researchers described how learning the programming skills required for making video games resulted in gains in mathematical thinking (Papanastasiou & Ferdig, 2006). High school students who used a modified video game, *Civiliza-*

tion IV, significantly improved their comprehension and retention of historical concepts (Moshirnia, 2007). These gains in achievement may be due to the fact that making video games requires students to become subject matter experts because they have to know the content well enough to teach others through their games (Ferdig, 2007).

These examples from recent studies provide both encouragement and research support for using new media in classrooms. These investigations demonstrate that using DIY media in the teaching-learning process is not a distraction from but a route to improving students' achievement. Researchers have illustrated how practice with these DIY media can lead to gains in students' attitudes, engagement, motivation, and understandings of content concepts and skills. Accordingly, we have shown how these new media texts and practices foster and require sophisticated new literacy skills and abilities and develop traditional literacy skills as well.

A succinct overview of the skills and abilities fostered by specific DIY media is provided in Appendix B. Although this is not a complete list of all of the literacy skills and abilities required by these practices, this summary does include those that were identified by researchers as they watched students interacting with and producing new media. We offer this overview as a way of encouraging our readers to try out these new textual forms and formats in their own instruction.

RESOURCES FOR USING DIY MEDIA IN CLASSROOM INSTRUCTION

We have also included a brief bibliography of resources related to teaching and learning with DIY media in Appendix A. We have included this list of sources as continued support for teachers who want to learn from others' experience and advice. This is not a comprehensive list, but rather a guide to some of the most recent publications, blogs, and websites that offer encouragement and guidance.

Finally, we invite our readers to visit our weblog at www.adolescentsdiy.blogspot.com. There we offer updates on new DIY media, links to recent research, and other suggestions for further information and support. We can be contacted through our blog to answer your questions or provide further assistance in promoting DIY media in content teaching. We've also established our blog as a space for you to share your own experiences in experimenting with these new media in your classroom as your journey with DIY media begins and progresses. We anticipate that you will find this an exciting adventure filled with pleasant surprises and enthusiastic responses. Please continue your journey by adding to our story of DIY media in content teaching.

Glossary

Anime—A stylized Japanese form of video animation.

Application—A platform for software developers to create games, tools, or other items for use on social networking platforms like Facebook or MySpace.

Art blog—Common type of blog that shares art, usually offering the ability of others to comment on or discuss it.

Avatar—The graphical representation of a computer user or persona, especially in a video game or virtual world.

Beatboxing—The art of imitating the sound of drumbeats and other musical sounds with one's voice.

Beta-reader—Someone who proofreads a fan fiction story for spelling, grammar, clarity, and consistency before the author shares it with the general community.

Blog—Shortened term for "weblog," a platform through which an individual person or a group of people can write about a variety of subjects in the form of posts, often for others to read.

Blogosphere—The universe of online blogging.

Canon—The body of material produced by the original creator or creators of a fictional universe, such as a book series or television show, that officially defines the setting, characters, and details of this world.

Character blogger—A person who maintains an online journal or profile on a social networking site from the point of view of a fictional character.

Chiptunes—Electronic music made by using the sound chips from video game consoles and computers, instead of traditional musical instruments and synthesizers.

Circuit bending—The practice of modifying electronic devices to create one-of-a kind musical instruments.

Comments—Messages User A sends as a reaction to User B's content, usually publicly viewable.

Community Technology Centers (CTCs)—Centers that offer free access for families to computers and the Internet.

Console—A machine designed solely for the purpose of playing video games.

Cosplay—Short for "costume roleplay," a type of performance art in which fans create and dress in costumes resembling their favorite characters.

Cover song—A song created and popularized by one artist that is reinterpreted and performed or recorded by another.

Criterion reference test—Tests that are not norm-referenced but are informal assessments or rubrics that provide information about an individual's performance.

Crowdsourcing—A neologism that refers to the farming out of tasks to a generally large network of amateurs rather than paid professionals.

Cyberbullying—Use of online applications to harass or taunt others, of specific concern to adolescents.

Cyberstalker—A person who monitors and harasses others online.

Digital migrant—A person who has not grown up with computers.

Digital native—A person who has grown up with computers.

Digital puppetry—User manipulation of characters in a video game or virtual world for the sake of machinima creation.

Distro—An online or mail order organization that distributes zines.

DIYers—Those who engage in do-it-yourself projects and create their own media or other products.

DIY media—Self-created digital or print media.

E-books—Books published and available to read online; some are free while others require payment.

Embedding—A process by which videos or other media can be posted and viewed on social networking platforms or other websites.

Emoticons—Typewritten symbols for emotions (e.g., smily faces).

Fan art—2D or 3D visual art inspired by fandom of a series.

Fan fiction—Creative writing based on the characters or universes of books, television shows, movies, comics, video games, and other fiction.

Fandom—The fan community of a particular work, including all websites, zines, and people devoted to it.

Freestyling—Improvised rhymes recited either unaccompanied or over music.

Friends—Other users accepted into a user's network, common on social networking sites and blogs that may determine if users can view one another's content.

Host—The platform that operates the software used to produce something online, e.g., blog-hosting sites or social networking sites.

Hypertextual stories—Text with embedded links to other pages of text, in order to tell a story.

Infoshop—A center that distributes radical political, usually anarchist, literature and information and can serve as a meeting place for local activist groups.

LAN gaming—A type of multiplayer gaming accomplished by connecting one or more computers directly to one another via a Local Area Network (LAN).

Machinima—Real-world filmmaking techniques applied within an interactive virtual space, often using 3D video game technologies where characters and events can be controlled either by humans, scripts, or artificial intelligence.

Manga—Japanese comic books and graphic novels, especially popular with adolescents.

Meme—Content that spreads rapidly via email, blogs, chat forums, social networking sites, etc.

Metaverse—A virtual world.

MMORPG—Massively multiplayer online role-playing games. Highly graphical two- or three-dimensional video games that allow individuals, through their self-created digital characters or avatars, to interact with the gaming software and with other players' avatars.

Modding—The process of altering features of video games or creating entirely new video games from existing games.

New literacies—New forms of literate practice, either print or digital.

Podcasts—Recordings available online for downloading.

Role-playing—The act of assuming the role of a fictional character, usually for the sake of gaming.

Slash fiction—A subgenre of fan fiction that centers on non-canon romantic and/or sexual relationships between characters. The term comes from the "/" symbol that is used to designate pairings, e.g., "Character A/ Character B."

Social media—A platform for sharing and discussion of information with a large audience.

Social networking—A platform to connect users to other users through online personal friendship networks and communities.

Sprite—An animation of a single character, object, or background from a video game.

Status updates—A feature that allows users to share short text messages with people in their social network, available on Facebook and MySpace and other social networking platforms.

Tweets—Text updates on the social networking site Twitter, limited to 140 characters.

Viral video—An online video that is seen by so many people that it becomes a pop culture phenomenon.

Web 2.0—New era of Internet usage beginning in the early 2000s and focused on sharing information, creating, collaborating, and networking.

Web comic—A comic that is distributed primarily online.

Wiki—Website software that allows the creation and sharing of interconnected pages, often used as a reference to share information collaboratively.

Zine—Small, self-published booklet containing material generated by amateur writers and artists.

Zinester—A person who creates or helps to create a zine.

Zining—The act of creating a zine.

Resources for Using DIY Media in Classrooms

The following is a short bibliography of some of the most recent and relevant books, articles, and online resources that teachers may find useful in incorporating DIY media into content teaching.

Books

Boss, S., Krauss, J., & Conery, L. (2008). *Reinventing project-based learning: Your field guide to real projects in the digital age.* Washington, DC: International Society for Technology in Education.

> This readable book addresses digital media in the classroom, offers examples from classrooms around the world, and includes a chapter on authentic assessment.

Braun, L. (2007). *Listen up! Podcasting for schools and libraries.* Medford, NJ: Information Today.

> This is a brief guide on how to podcast and where to find the resources to do so.

Nicholson, W. (2008). *Blogs, wikis, podcasts and other powerful web tools for classrooms* (2nd ed.). Thousand Oaks, CA: Corwin Press.

> This is a guide to integrating digital media, including Flickr, into the classroom. Firsthand classroom experience is coupled with updated research and information on Internet safety and information literacy.

Robbins, S., & Bell, M. (2007). *Second Life for dummies.* Hoboken, NJ: Wiley.

> This guide to the virtual world of *Second Life* provides direction for navigating and creating n this virtual world and includes a discussion of *Teen Second Life*.

Solomon, G., & Schrum, L. S. (2007). *Web 2.0: New tools, new schools.* Washington, DC: International Society for Technology in Education.

> This book reviews digital tools, including wikis, blogs, and podcasts, and discusses the place that technology should take in schools.

Warlick, D. (2008). *Classroom blogging* (2nd ed.). Lulu.com.

> This is a teacher's guide to blogs, wikis, and other media tools.

Web Resources

Readwriteweb.com (www.readwriteweb.com)

> This is a blog that provides daily updates on technologies. It includes reviews of Technologies and news about technologies such as Facebook, Twitter, and LiveJournal, and lists the most popular YouTube videos.

Media Awareness Network (www.media-awareness.ca/English/index. cfm)

> This site offers resources and support for teachers interested in media literacy.

eHow.com (www.eHow.com)

> This site promotes the DIY ethic by providing directions for how to do just about everything, such as how to download a podcast and how to burn a CD or DVD.

Literacy Skills in Various Forms of DIY Media

	Blogs	Social Networking Sites	Video Games	Machinima	Virtual Worlds	YouTube and Video Sharing Sites	Wikis
Making intertextual ties	X	X	X	X	X		X
Writing hybrid texts	X	X	X	X	X	X	X
Integrating graphics	X			X		X	X
Evaluating texts	X	X	X		X	X	X
Writing in a genre	X		X	X	X		X
Developing story elements	X			X			
Understanding semiotic domains			X		X		
Reading multimodal texts			X	X	X		
Reading visual cues		X	X		X	X	
Reading linguistic cues			X		X		
Making generalizations	X		X		X		X
Drawing conclusions			X		X		
Understanding complex vocabulary	X		X		X		
Analyzing text	X		X		X		X
Interpreting multiple and simultaneous information	X		X		X		X
Reading hybrid texts	X		X		X		X
Understanding abbreviations	X	X	X		X		X
Taking critical perspectives			X	X	X		
Interpreting sign systems and graphics	X		X		X		

	Resource-Sharing Sites	Fan Art	Fan Fiction	Comics	Zines	Indie Music	Digital Story-telling	Pod-casting	Ani-mations
Making intertextual ties	X		X	X	X		X		X
Writing hybrid texts	X		X	X	X		X		X
Integrating graphics		X			X				
Evaluating texts	X								
Writing in a genre	X			X	X				
Developing story elements		X	X	X			X		X
Understanding semiotic domains			X						X
Reading mulitimodal texts									
Reading visual cues			X	X			X		X
Reading linguistic cues	X								
Making generalizations									
Drawing conclusions									
Understanding complex vocabulary									
Analyzing text	X			X					X
Interpreting multiple and simultaneous information									
Reading hybrid texts	X								
Understanding abbreviations	X								
Taking critical perspectives		X				X			
Interpreting sign systems and graphics				X					X

	Blogs	Social Networking Sites	Video Games	Machinima	Virtual Worlds	YouTube and Video Sharing Sites	Wikis
Producing collaborative knowledge			X		X		
Use new information			X		X		X
Locate information		X					
Blend multimedia elements		X		X		X	X
Writing for a specific audience	X	X					
Interpreting literary devices	X						
Decode meaning systems			X		X		
Read for problem solving			X		X		
Reflective thinking			X		X	X	
Metacognitive thinking			X		X		
Writing in nonlinear forms				X			X
Understanding viewpoints							X
Crafting intricate plots				X			X
Changing voice							
Editing				X			
Blending genres							
Learning computational ideas				X			
Learning design skills				X			
Storytelling abilities				X		X	
Deconstructing texts							
Creative writing				X			
Transposing written to oral text							

	Resource-Sharing Sites	Fan Art	Fan Fiction	Comics	Zines	Indie Music	Digital Story-telling	Pod-casting	Ani-mations
Producing collaborative knowledge	X			X		X			X
Use new information	X							X	
Locate information	X								
Blend multimedia elements		X							
Writing for a specific audience						X		X	
Interpreting literary devices									
Decode meaning systems									
Read for problem solving									
Reflective thinking	X	X				X		X	
Metacognitive thinking						X	X		
Writing in nonlinear forms						X			
Understanding viewpoints	X								
Crafting intricate plots									
Changing voice			X	X			X		X
Editing			X	X			X	X	X
Blending genres			X	X	X		X		X
Learning computational ideas			X						X
Learning design skills		X							
Storytelling abilities						X			X
Deconstructing texts					X		X		
Creative writing			X	X	X	X	X		X
Transposing written to oral text						X		X	

References

Alverez, D. (1998). Four adolescents, their compensatory strategies and writing development and the texts they authored out of school [Doctoral dissertation, University of Wisconsin, 1990]. *Dissertation Abstracts International, 59,* 2478.

Alvermann, D. E. (2002). *Adolescents and literacies in a digital world.* New York: Peter Lang.

Alvermann, D. E. (2009). Sociocultural constructions of adolescence and young people's literacies. In L. Christenbury, R. Bomber, & P. Smagorinsky (Ed.), *Handbook of adolescent literacy research* (pp. 14–28). New York: Guilford Press.

Anagnostopoulos, D. (2003). Testing and student engagement with literature in urban classrooms: A multi-layered perspective. *Research in the Teaching of English, 38,* 177–212.

Anderson Analytics. (2008, December 1). *Blogging increasing in popularity among generation Y.* Retrieved September 20, 2009, from www.anderson analytics.com

Anderson, C. (2003, October). *Violent video games: Myths, facts and unanswered questions.* Retrieved July 25, 2009, from http://www.apa.org/science/psa/sb-anderson.html

BBC News. (2006, November 27). *Star Wars* kid is top video. *BBC News.* Retrieved July 28, 2009, from http://news.bbc.co.uk/2/hi/entertainment/6187554.stm

Bean, T. W., Bean, S. K., & Bean, K. F. (1998). Intergenerational conversations and two adolescents' multiple literacies: Implications for redefining content area literacy. *Journal of Adolescent and Adult Literacy, 41,* 508–517.

Bitz, M. (2004). The comic book project: Forging alternative pathways to literacy. *Journal of Adolescent and Adult Literacy, 47*(7), 574–586.

Black, R. (2008). Language, culture and identity in online fanfiction. *E-Learning, 3*(2), 170–184.

Black, R., & Steinkuehler, C. (2009). Literacy in virtual worlds. In L. Christenbury, R. Bomber, & P. Smagorinsky (Eds.), *Handbook of adolescent literacy research* (pp. 271–286). New York: Guilford Press.

Blair, H., & Sanford, K. (2004). Morphing literacy: Boys reshaping their school-based literacy practices. *Language Arts, 81*(6), 452–460. Retrieved September 19, 2009, from http://www.wired.com/politics/onlinerights/news/2007/08/wiki_tracker

Borland, J. (2007, August 14). *Wired.* Retrieved October 26, 2009, from http://www.wired.com/politics/onlinerights/news/2007/08/wikitracker

Botzakis, S. (2008). "I've gotten a lot out of reading comics": Poaching and lifelong literacy. In Y. Kim, V. J. Risko, D. L. Compton, D. K. Dickinson, M. K. Hundley, R. T. Jimenez, K. M. Leander, & D. W. Rowe (Eds.), *57th yearbook of the National Reading Conference* (pp. 119–129). Oak Creek, WI: National Reading Conference.

Burke, A., & Rowsell, J. (2007). Assessing multimodal learning practices. *E-Learning, 4*(1), 329–342.

Carvin, A. (2000). Mind the gap: The digital divide as the new civil rights issue of the new millennium. *Multimedia Schools, 1*(1), 56–58.

Cassell, J., & Jenkins, H. (1998). *From Barbie to* Mortal Kombat: *Gender and computer games.* Cambridge, MA: MIT Press.

Chandler-Olcott, K., & Mahar, D. (2003). Adolescents anime inspired fanfictions: An exploration of multiliteracies. *Journal of Adolescent and Adult Literacy, 46*(7), 556–566.

Cherland, M. (2009). What does Harry Potter have to say about girls? *Journal of Adolescent and Adult Literacy, 52*(4), 273–382.

Collis, S. (2009, April). *Practical examples of 3D virtual environments for learning in high school.* Retrieved July 23, 2009, from http://www.happysteve.com/2009/04/pratical-examples-of-3d-virtual-environments

Conley, M. (2008). Literacy assessment for adolescents: What's fair about it? In K. A. Hinchman & H. K. Sheridan-Thomas (Eds.), *Best practices in adolescent literacy instruction* (pp. 297–312). New York: Guilford Press.

Datman, E. (2005). Make way for wikis. *School Library Journal, 51*(11), 52–54.

Dean, C. (2007, April 17). Computer science takes steps to bring women to the fold. *The New York Times.* Retrieved July 27, 2009, from http://www.nytimes.com/2007/04/17/science/17comp.html?ex=1185163200&en=9d6945

Denner, J., Werner, L., Bean, S., & Campe, S. (2005). The Girls Creating Games program: Strategies for engaging middle school girls in information technology. *Frontiers: A Journal of Women's Studies, 26*(1), 90–98.

Desmond, R. (1987). Adolescents and music lyrics: Implications of a cognitive perspective. *Communication Quarterly, 35,* 276–284.

Dobner, V. (2004, April 7). *Surgeons may err less by playing video games.* Retrieved July 27, 2009, from http://ww.msnbc.msn.com/id/4685909/

Duffy, P. D., & Bruns, A. (2006, September 26). *The use of blogs, wikis and RSS in education: A conversation of possibilities.* Online Learning and Teaching Conference, Brisbane, Australia. Retrieved August 2, 2009, from http://sprints.qut.edu/au/5398/

Duncan-Andrade, J. M. R., & Morrell, E. (2000, April). *Using hip-hop culture as a bridge to canonical poetry texts in an urban secondary English class.* Paper presented at the annual meeting of the American Educational Research Association, New Orleans.

Ferdig, R. E. (2007, October 25). Can game development impact academic achievement? *THE Journal: Transforming Education through Technology.* Retrieved September 21, 2009, from http://thejournal.com/Articles/2007/10/25/can-game-development-impact-academic-achievement?

Fox, S., & Madden, M. (2006). *Generations online.* Washington, DC: Pew Internet and American Life Project. Retrieved July 23, 2009, from www.pewinternet.org/PPF/r/170/report_display.asp

Gasmo, H. (2004). *Computing: Excludingly boring at school, includingly cool at home.* Retrieved July 10, 2009, from http:www.sigis-ist.org

Gaudin, S. (2009, June 16). Facebook dethrones MySpace in U.S. popularity race. *ComputerWorld.* Retrieved September 20, 2009, from www.computerworld.com/s/article/9134463/Facebook_dethrones_MySpace_in_U.S._popularity_race

Gee, J. P. (2003). *What video games have to teach us about learning and literacy.* New York: Palgrave/Macmillan.

Gee, J. P., Hull, G., & Lankshear, C. (1996). *The new work order: Behind the language of the new capitalism.* Boulder, CO: Westview.

Giles, J. (2005, December 15). Special report: Internet encyclopedias go head to head. *Nature, 438,* 900–901. Retrieved August 1, 2009, from http://www.nature.com/nature/journal/v438/n7070/full/438900a.html

Gonzales, N., Moll, L. C., & Amanti, C. (2005). *Funds of knowledge: Theorizing practices in homes and classrooms.* New York: Erlbaum.

Goodwin, M. H. (2007). *He said—she said: Talk as social organization among black children.* Bloomington: Indiana University Press.

Green, B. (1997, July). *Literacy, information and the learning society.* Keynote address to the joint conference of the Australian Association for the Teaching of English, the Australian Literacy Educators' Association, and the Australian School Library Association, Darwin High School, Northern Territory, Australia.

Greenaway, P. (2001). Media and arts education: A global view from Australia. In R. Kubey (Ed.), *Media literacy in the information age: Current perspectives* (Vol. 6, pp. 187–198). New Brunswick, NJ: Transaction Publishers.

Guzzetti, B. J. (2008). Identities in online communities: A young woman's critique of cyberculture. *E-Learning, 5*(3), 457–474.

Guzzetti, B. J. (2009a). Adolescents' explorations with do-it-yourself media: Authoring identity in out of school settings. In M. C. Hagood (Ed.), *New literacies practices: Designing literacy learning* (pp. 41–59). New York: Peter Lang.

Guzzetti, B. J. (2009b). Lessons on literacy learning and teaching: Listening to adolescent girls. In L. Christenbury, R. Bomber, & P. Smagorinsky (Eds.), *Handbook of research on adolescent literacy* (pp. 372–385). New York: Guilford Press.

Guzzetti, B. J. (2009c). Thinking like a forensic scientist: Learning with academic and everyday texts. *Journal of Adolescent and Adult Literacy, 53*(3), 192–203.

Guzzetti, B. J., & Gamboa, M. (2004). Zining: The unsanctioned literacy practice of adolescents. In C. Fairbanks, J. Worthy, B. Maloch, J. Hoffman, & D. L. Schallert (Eds.), *53rd yearbook of the National Reading Conference* (pp. 206–217). Oak Creek, WI: National Reading Conference.

Guzzetti, B. J., & Gamboa, M. (2005a). Online journaling: The informal writings of two adolescent girls. *Research in the Teaching of English, 40,* 168–206.

Guzzetti, B. J., & Gamboa, M. (2005b). Zines for social justice: Adolescent girls writing on their own. *Reading Research Quarterly, 39*(4), 408–435.

Guzzetti, B. J., & Yang, Y. (2005). Adolescents' punk rock fandom: Construction and production of lyrical texts. In B. Maloch, J. V. Hoffman, D. L. Schallert, C. M. Fairbanks, & J. Worthy (Eds.), *54th yearbook of the National Reading Conference* (pp. 198–210). Oak Creek, WI: National Reading Conference.

Habgood, M., Ainsworth, S., & Benford, S. (2005). Endogenous fantasy and learning in digital games. *Simulation & Gaming, 36*(4), 483.

Hammett, R. F. (2007). Assessment and new literacies. *E-Learning, 4*(3), 343–354.

Hayes, E. R., & Games, I. A. (2008). Making computer games and design thinking. *Games and Culture, 3*(3–4), 309–332.

Hefferman, V. (2007, April 19). The WEB: Online, students say reach out to loners. *New York Times* online. Retrieved July 25, 2009, from www.nytimes.com/2007/04/19/arts/19scre.html

Helmond, A. (2008, February 11). How many blogs are there? Is someone still counting? *The Blog Herald.* Retrieved July 14, 2009, from http://www.blogherald.com/2008/02/11/how-many-blogs-are-there?

Herring, S. C. (2001, October). *Gender and power in online communication.* Retrieved June 30, 2009, from http://rkesi.indiiana.edu/archive/CSI/WP/WP01-05B.html

Howe, J. (2006, June 2). The rise of crowdsourcing. *Wired, 14*(6). Retrieved July 24, 2009, from http://www.wired.com/wired/archive/14.06/crowds.html

Huffacker, D. (2005). The educated blogger: Using weblogs to promote literacy in the classroom. *AACE Journal, 13*(20), 91–98.

Hull, G., & Schultz, K. (Eds.). (2002). *School's out! Bridging out of school literacies with classroom practice.* New York: Teachers College Press.

Hyer, T. (2006, May). Intro to design thinking: An interview with David Burney. *Red Hat Magazine,* 19. Retrieved November 7, 2009, from http://www.redhat.com/magazine/019may06/features/burney

Hyman, P. (2004). *Video game companies encourage "modders."* Retrieved July 27, 2009, from http://www/hollywoodreporter.com/hr/search/articledisplay.jsp?

Intrator, S. M., & Kunzman, R. (2009). Who are adolescents today: Youth voices and what they tell us. In L. Christenbury, R. Bomber, & P. Smagorinksy (Eds.), *Handbook of adolescent literacy research* (pp. 29–45). New York: Guilford Press.

Jenkins, H. (2006). *Fans, bloggers, and gamers: Exploring participatory culture.* New York: New York University Press.

Johnson, S. B. (2005). *Everything bad is good for you: How today's popular culture is actually making us smarter.* New York: Riverhead/Penguin Books.

Jones, S. (2003). *Let the games begin: Gaming technology and entertainment among college students.* Retrieved July 26, 2009, from www.pew internet.org/reports/toc.asp?Report=93

Kafai, Y. B. (1995). *Minds in play: Computer game design as a context for children's learning.* Mahwah, NJ: Erlbaum.

Kafai, Y. B. (2006). Playing and making games for learning: Instructionist and constructionist perspectives for game studies. *Games and Culture, 1*(1), 36.

Kafai, Y. B., Franke, M., Ching, C., & Shih, J. (2008). Game design as an interactive learning environment for fostering students and teachers mathematical inquiry. *International Journal of Computers for Mathematical Learning, 3*(2), 149–184.

Kearney, M. C. (2006a). *Girls make media.* New York: Routledge.

Kearney, M. C. (2006b). Prospective science teachers as e-learning designers. *Australian Journal of Educational Technology, 22*(2), 229–250.

Kelly, D., Pomerantz, S., & Currie, D. H. (2006). "No boundaries?" Girls' interactive, online learning about femininities. *Youth & Society, 38*(1), 3–28.

Kist, W. (2003). Student achievement in new literacies for the 21st century. *Middle School Journal, 36*(1), 6–13.

Kist, W. (2005). *New literacies in action: Learning and teaching in multiple media.* New York: Teachers College Press.

Knobel, M. (2001). "I'm not a pencil man": How one student challenges our notions of literacy failure in school. *Journal of Adolescent and Adult Literacy, 44*(5), 405–414.

Knobel, M., & Lankshear, C. (2001). Cut, paste, publish: The production and consumption of zines. In D. E. Alvermann (Ed.), *Adolescents and literacies in a digital world* (pp. 164–185). New York: Peter Lang.

Lang, P. G. (2008). Publicly private and privately public: Social networking on YouTube. *Journal of Computer-Mediated Communication, 13*(1), article 18. Retrieved November 6, 2009, from http://jcmc.indiana.edu/vol13/issue1/lange.html

Lankshear, C., & Knobel, M. (2003). *New literacies: Changing knowledge and classroom learning.* Buckingham, England: Open University Press.

Leland, C. H., Harste, J. C., & Kuonen, K. (2008). Unpacking videogames: Understanding and supporting a new ethos. In Y. Kim, V. J. Risko, D. L. Compton, M. K. Hundley, R. T. Jimenez, K. M. Leander, & D. W. Rowe (Eds.), *57th yearbook of the National Reading Conference* (pp. 231–243). Oak Creek, WI: National Reading Conference.

Lenhart, A. (2007). *Pew Internet & American life project: Data memo.* Retrieved April 13, 2008, from http://www.pweintnet.org/PPF/r/230/report_display.asp

Lenhart, A., & Fox, S. (2006). *Bloggers: A portrait of the Internet's new story-tellers.* Washington, DC: Pew Internet and American Life Project. Retrieved June 30, 2009, from www.pewinternet.org/PPF/r/186/reprot_display.asp

Lenhart, A., Kahne, J., Middaugh, E., Macgill, A., Evans, C., & Vitak, J. (2008, September 16). *Teens, video games and civics* [Pew Internet & American Life Project]. Retrieved July 26, 2009, from http://www.pewinternet.org/Reports/200/Teens-Video_Games-and-civics.

Lenhart, A., & Madden, M. (2005). *Teen content creators and consumers.* Washington, DC: Pew Internet and American Life Project.

Lenhart, A., Madden, M., Smith, A., & Macgill, A. (2007, December 17). *Teens and social media* [Pew Internet and American Life Project]. Retrieved September 20, 2009, from http://www.pewinternet.org/Reports/2007/Teens-and-Social-Media.aspx

Leu, D., Kinzer, C., Corio, J., & Cammak, D. (2004). Toward a theory of new literacies emerging from the Internet and other information technologies. In R. B. Ruddell & N. J. Unrau (Eds.), *Theoretical models and processes of reading* (pp. 1570–1613). Newark, DE: International Reading Association.

Lewis, C., Leander, K., & Wang, X. (2008). Digital literacies. In B. J. Guzzetti (Ed.), *Literacy for the new millennium: Adolescent literacy* (pp. 207–222). Westport, CT: Praeger.

Lidetke, M. (2007, March 5). Web pioneer touts Ning.Inc as easy to use social network. *The Rocky Mountain News.* Retrieved September 9, 2009, from http://www.rockymountainnews.com/drmn/tech/article/0,2777.RMN_23910_5394821,00.html

Luce-Kapler, R. (2007). Radical change and wikis: Teaching new literacies. *Journal of Adolescent and Adult Literacy, 51*(3), 214–223.

Luce-Kapler, R., & Dobson, T. (2005, May/June). In search of a story: Reading and writing e-literature. *Reading Online, 8*(6). Retrieved December 21, 2009, from www.readingonline.org/articles/art_index.asp?HREF=luce-kapler/index.html

Luke, A. (2003). Pedagogy, community, multimodality, and interdisciplinarity. *Reading Research Quarterly, 38,* 397–403.

Magnifico, A. (2005, March). *Science, literacy and the Internet? Epistemic games: Building the future of education.* Retrieved June 8, 2009, from http://www.epistemicgames.org/eg/?p=463

Mahiri, J. (Ed.). (2004). *What they don't learn in school: Literacy in the lives of urban youth.* New York: Peter Lang.

Majors, Y., Kim, J., & Ansari, S. (2009). Beyond hip-hop: A cultural context view of literacy. In L. Christenbury, R. Bomber, & P. Smagorinsky (Eds.), *Handbook of adolescent literacy research* (pp. 343–359). New York: Guilford Press.

Marshall, J. (2009). Divided against ourselves: Standards, assessments, and adolescent literacy. In L. Christenbury, R. Bomber, & P. Smagorinsky (Eds.), *Handbook of adolescent literacy research* (pp. 113–125). New York: Guilford Press.

Mazzarella, S. R. (2005). *Girl wide web: Girls, the Internet and negotiation of identity.* New York: Peter Lang.

McClay, J. K., Mackey, M., Carbonaro, M., Szafron, D., & Schaeffer, J. (2007). Adolescents composing fiction in digital game and written formats: Tacit, explicit and metacognitive strategies. *E-Learning, 4*(3), 273–284.

Morrell, E., & Duncan-Andrade, J. M. R. (2008). Promoting academia literacy with urban youth through engaging hip-hop culture. *The English Journal, 91*(6), 88–92.

Moshirnia, A. (2007). The educational potential of modified video games. *Issues in Informing Science and Information Technology, 4*, 511–521.

Nakashima, E. (2007, April 30). Sexual threats quiet some female bloggers. *The Washington Post.* Retrieved June 28, 2009, from http://www.azcentral.com/offbeat/articles/0430femalebloggers-ON.html

Norton, B. (2003). The motivating power of comic books: Insights from *Archie* comic readers. *The Reading Teacher, 57*(2), 140–147.

Nussbaum, B. (2005, March). The empathy economy. *Business Week.* Retrieved July 27, 2009, from http://www.businessweek.com/bwdaily/dnfalsh/mar2005/nf2005037_4086.htm

Papanastasiou, E. C., & Ferdig, R. E. (2006). Computer use and mathematical literacy: An analysis of existing and potential relationships. *Journal of Computers in Mathematics and Science Teaching, 25*(4), 361–371.

Penrod, D. (2007). *Using blogs to enhance literacy: The next powerful step in 21st century learning.* Lanham, MD: Rowman & Littlefield.

Peppler, K. A., & Kafai, Y. B. (2007a). From SuperGoo to Scratch: Exploring creative digital media production in informal learning. *Learning, Media and Technology, 32*(2), 149–166.

Peppler, K., & Kafai, Y. B. (2007b). What videogame making can teach us about literacy and learning: Alternative pathways into participatory culture. In A. Baba (Ed.), *Situated play: Proceedings of the Third International Conference of the Digital Games Research Association* (pp. 369–376). Tokyo, Japan.

Prensky, M. (2006). *"Don't bother me Mom—I'm learning!"* St. Paul, MN: Paragon House.

Rhodes, J. A., & Robnolt, V. J. (2009). Digital literacies in the classroom. In L. Christenbury, R. Bomber, & P. Smagorinsky (Eds.), *Handbook of adolescent literacy research* (pp 153–169). New York: Guilford Press.

Robertson, J., & Good, J. (2004). Children's narrative development through computer game authoring. In A. Druin (Ed.), *Proceedings of the 2004 conference on interaction design and children: Building a community* (pp. 57–64). New York: Association for Computing Machinery. Retrieved November 6, 2009, from http://www.idc2004.org

Row, H. (1997). *From fandom to feminism: An analysis of the zine press.* Retrieved August 2, 2009, from http://www.zinebook.com/resource/heath.html

Rubinstein-Avilla, E. (2007). In their words, sounds and images: After-school literacy programs for urban youth. In B. J. Guzzetti (Ed.),

Literacy for the new millennium: Adolescent literacy (pp. 239–250). West-port, CT: Praeger.

Rubinstein-Avilia, E. (2009). Reflecting on the challenges of conducting research across national and linguistic borders: Lessons from the field. *Journal of Language and Literacy Education, 5*(2), 1–8. Retrieved November 6, 2009, from http://wqqww.coe.uga.edu/jolle/2009_1/reflecting.pdf

Salinger, T. (2007). Adolescent literacy assessment. In B. J. Guzzetti (Ed.), *Literacy for the new millennium: Adolescent literacy* (pp. 53–72). West-port, CT: Praeger.

Sanders, B. (1995). *A is for ox: The collapse of literacy and the rise of violence in an electronic age.* New York: Random House.

Sanford, K., & Madill, L. (2007). Critical literacy learning through video games: Adolescent boys' perspectives. *E-Learning, 4*(3), 285–296.

Santa, C. (2006). A vision for adolescent literacy: Ours or theirs? *Journal of Adolescent and Adult Literacy, 49*(6), 478–488.

Schultz, K., Vasudevan, L., & Throop, R. (2007). Adolescent literacy toward global citizenship. In B. J. Guzzetti (Ed.), *Literacy for the new millennium: Adolescent literacy* (pp. 21–36). Westport, CT: Praeger.

Schwartz, A., & Rubinstein-Avilla, E. (2006). Understanding the manga hype: Uncovering the multimodality of comic book literacies. *Journal of Adolescent and Adult Literacy, 50*(1), 40–49.

Scott, J. (2008, May). *Gather no dust: The public access computer problem.* Retrieved July 13, 2009, from http://gathjernodust.blogspot.com/2008/05/public_access_computer_problem

Skelton, C. (2001). *Schooling the boys: Masculinities and primary education.* Buckingham, UK: Open University Press.

Squire, K., Giovanetto, L., Devane, B., & Durga, S. (2005). From users to designers: Building a self-organizing game-based learning environment. *TechTrends, 49*(5), 34–43.

Steinkuehler, C. (2007). Massively multiplayer online gaming as a constellation of literacy practices. *E-Learning, 4*(3), 297–318.

Steward, T. (March, 2007). *Blogs, wikis and social networks for adolescents.* Retrieved July 24, 2009, from http://www.tonystreardblog.com/2007/03/11/blogs-wikis-and-social

Street, B. V. (1995). *Social literacies: Critical approaches to literacy in development, ethnography and education.* London: Longmore.

Street, B. V. (2005). Recent applications of new literacy studies in educational contexts. *Research in the Teaching of English, 39*(4), 417–423.

Subrahmanyam, K., Smahel, D., & Greenfield, P. (2006). Connecting developmental constructions to the Internet: Identity presentation and sexual exploration in online teen chat rooms. *Developmental Psychology, 42,* 395–406.

Szalai, G., & Uni, C. (2009, June 25). Teens making time for digital and traditional media. *Media Week.* Retrieved July 28, 2009, from http://www.mediaweek.com/MW/content_display/news/digital_download/metrics/e3i4993a5c32cf65e036396027aC8bbb59

Tapscott, D. (1998). *Growing up digital: The rise of the net generation.* New York: McGraw-Hill.

Technorati. (2008). *State of the blogosphere.* Retrieved September 20, 2009, from http://technorati.com/blogging/state-of-the-blogosphere

Thomas, A. (2005). Digital literacies of the cybergirl. *E-Learning, 1*(1), 358–382.

Thomas, A. (2007). Breaking through the boundaries of narrative, literacy, and identity in adolescent fan fiction. In M. Knobel & C. Lankshear (Eds.), *A new literacies sampler* (pp. 137–166). New York: Peter Lang.

Warren, F. (2005). *Postsecret.* New York: HarperCollins/Regan.

Warren, F. (2006). *My secret: A postsecret book.* New York: William Morrow/HarperCollins.

Warren, S. J., Dondlinger, M. J., & Barab, S. A. (2008). A MUVE towards PBL writing: Effects of a digital learning environment designed to improve elementary student writing. *Journal of Research in Technology in Education, 41*(1), 113–140.

Wearden, G. (2001, August 20). Researchers: Video games hurt brain development. *CNET News.* Retrieved November, 6, 2009, from http://news.com/Researchers+Video+games+hurt+brain+development/2100-1040_3-271849.html

Weber, B. (2004, July 8). Fewer noses stuck in books in America, survey finds. *The New York Times,* p. E1.

Weekly Reader Know Your World Extra. (2007, February 23). *Web of Lies, 40,* 6–7.

Wilbur, D. (2008). ilife: Understanding and connecting to the digital literacies of adolescents. In K. A. Hinchman & H. K. Sheridan (Eds.), *Best practices in adolescent literacy instruction: Solving problems in the teaching of literacy* (pp. 57–77). New York: Guilford Press.

Wolsey, T. D., & Grisham, D. L. (2007). Adolescents and the new literacies: Writing engagement. *Action in Teacher Education, 29*(2), 29–36.

Xu, S. H. (2008). Rethinking literacy learning and teaching: Intersections of adolescents' in-school and out-of-school literacy practices. In K. A. Hinchman & H. K. Sheridan (Eds.), *Best practices in adolescent literacy instruction* (pp. 39–56). New York: Guilford Press.

Young, J. R. (2006, June 12). The wired campus. *The Chronicle of Higher Education.* Retrieved September 20, 2009, from http://chronicle/blogspot/wikipedia-founder-discourages/2305

Index

Academy of Machinima Arts and
    Sciences, 38
Achievement, 84–85
Active Worlds (virtual world), 38
Adobe Flash video technology, 39, 44
Adolescence
    blogging and, 13–14
    creating video games and virtual
        worlds, 31–32, 33–37
    defining, xviii
    fan fiction/fan art/comics and, 64–67
    social networking and, 22–26
    teacher interest in DIY media and, 2–4
    zines and, 71
AdventureAuthor (video game), 36–37
After School Corporation, 7
After-school programs, 7
Ainsworth, S., 37
Alverez, D., 44
Alvermann, Donna, xviii, xx, 2, 9, 23
Amanti, C., 2
Anagnostopoulos, D., 80
Anderson, C., 32–33
Anderson Analytics, 12
Anderson Cooper 360, 45–46
Animations, 39, 44, 60, 95, 97
Anime, 60
Ansari, S., 72
APIs (Application Program Interfaces),
    48
Applications, in social networking/social
    media sites, 23
Art
    fan art, 61–62, 64–67, 95, 97
    social networking/social media sites
        in, 28
    video sharing and, 49

Assessment, 80–82
    informal, 81–82
    standardized, 80–81
Atari 2600 game system, 74–75
Authoring services, 12–13
Avatars, xx, 38

Balla, Lance, 76
Barab, S. A., 84
BBC News, 46
Bean, K. F., 81
Bean, S. K., 35–36, 81
Bean, T. W., 81
Bell, M., 91
Benford, S., 37
Beta-readers, 61
Bitz, M., 66
Black, R., 39, 65–66
Bloggers, 12, 16, 17
Blog-hosting sites, 12–13, 14
Blogosphere, 11–12, 17
Blogs, 3, 11–19
    adolescent use of, 13–14
    blog-hosting sites, 12–13, 14
    in classrooms, 16–19
    in content areas, 18–19
    literacy skills and abilities and, 18–19,
        94, 96
    nature of, 11–12
    privacy of, 14
    safety of, 14
    types of, 14–16
    video blogging, 48
    video sharing in, 44
Borland, J., 53
Boss, S., 91
Botzakis, S., 66

109

About the Authors

Barbara Guzzetti is a Professor in the division of Learning, Technology and Psychology in the Mary Lou Fulton Research Institute and Graduate School of Education at Arizona State University. She is also an affiliated faculty member in Women's and Gender Studies in the College of Liberal Arts and Sciences. Her recent interests in research and teaching focus on adolescents' new literacies, particularly digital literacies, and the gender and social justice issues that impact DIY media consumption and production. She enjoys learning new digital literacies from young people and colleagues. As a rescuer of Havanese and Bichon Frise dogs, she plans to use her DIY digital skills to create a virtual site for these breeds' rescue volunteers and donors at the dog park in *Second Life*.

Kate Elliott graduated in 2006 from Arizona State University with a Bachelor's degree in history and is a current graduate student in nonprofit studies at ASU. She is employed as the Staff Training and Volunteer Coordinator for Planned Parenthood Arizona. She is an avid user of online media tools like Twitter and social networking sites like Facebook and regularly reads blogs. Kate produced several issues of a zine as a teenager and continues to enjoy reading the work of other zinesters. She is currently exploring ways to use online social networking tools to organize volunteers and inform others about critical issues in the nonprofit sector.

Diana Welsch is a 2007 graduate of Arizona State University with a Bachelor's degree in Fine Arts with a minor in Chicana/o Studies. She currently works as a Library Assistant in a large urban public library where she develops and implements art, music, and gaming programs for teens. She has played guitar, bass, and drums in bands since she was 15, most recently as the bassist for *The Cullens*, a surf-punk tribute to the movie *Twilight*. She volunteers as a live sound engineer for local DIY art and music venues, reads an average of 50 books a year, and creates original visual and musical art when the muse moves her.